PEIRCE FOR ARCHITECTS

Ideas gain legitimacy as they are put to some practical use. A study of Charles Sanders Peirce (1839–1914) supports this pragmatism as a way of thinking about truth and meaning. Architecture has a strong pragmatic strand, not least as we think of building users, architecture as a practice, the practical demands of building, and utility. After all, Vitruvius placed firmness and delight in the company of *utilitas* amongst his demands on architecture.

Peirce (pronounced 'purse') was a logician, and so many of his ideas are couched in terms of formal propositions and their limitations. His work appeals therefore to many architects grappling with the digital age, and references to his work cropped up in the Design Methods Movement that developed and grew from the 1950s. That movement sought to systematise the design process, contributing to the idea of the RIBA Plan of Work, computer-aided design, and various controversies about rendering the design process transparent and open to scrutiny.

Peirce's commitment to logic led him to investigate the basic elements of logical statements, notably the element of the *sign*. His best-known contribution to design revolves around his intricate theory of semiotics, the science of signs. The study of semiotics divided around the 1980s between advocates of Peirce's semiotics, and the broader, more politically charged field of structuralism. The latter has held sway in architectural discourse since the 1980s. Why this happened and what we gain by reviving a Peircean semiotics is the task of this book.

Richard Coyne is Professor of Architectural Computing in the Edinburgh School of Architecture and Landscape Architecture at the University of Edinburgh. He was formerly Head of the School of Arts, Culture and Environment. He inaugurated the MSc in Design and Digital Media, and is Programme Director of the MSc by Research in Digital Media and Culture. He researches and teaches in architectural theory, design theory and digital technologies, and is author of ten books that include *Interpretation in Architecture: Design as a Way of Thinking* (with Adrian Snodgrass, 2006), *Derrida for Architects* (2011), *The Tuning of Place: Sociable Spaces and Pervasive Digital Media* (2010) and *Network Nature: The Place of Nature in the Digital Age* (2018).

Thinkers for Architects

Series Editor: Adam Sharr, Newcastle University, UK

Editorial Board

Jonathan A. Hale, University of Nottingham, UK
Hilde Heynen, KU Leuven, Netherlands
David Leatherbarrow, University of Pennsylvania, USA

> Architects have often looked to philosophers and theorists from beyond the discipline for design inspiration or in search of a critical framework for practice. This original series offers quick, clear introductions to key thinkers who have written about architecture and whose work can yield insights for designers.

'Each unintimidatingly slim book makes sense of the subjects' complex theories.'

Building Design

'… a valuable addition to any studio space or computer lab.'

Architectural Record

'… a creditable attempt to present their subjects in a useful way.'

Architectural Review

Goodman for Architects
Remei Capdevila-Werning

Merleau-Ponty for Architects
Jonathan Hale

Lefebvre for Architects
Nathaniel Coleman

Kant for Architects
Diane Morgan

Virilio for Architects
John Armitage

Peirce for Architects
Richard Coyne

THINKERS FOR ARCHITECTS

Peirce
for
Architects

Richard Coyne

LONDON AND NEW YORK

First published 2019
by Routledge
2 Park Square, Milton Park, Abingdon, Oxon OX14 4RN

and by Routledge
52 Vanderbilt Avenue, New York, NY 10017

Routledge is an imprint of the Taylor & Francis Group, an informa business

© 2019 Richard Coyne

The right of Richard Coyne to be identified as author of this work has been asserted by him in accordance with sections 77 and 78 of the Copyright, Designs and Patents Act 1988.

All rights reserved. No part of this book may be reprinted or reproduced or utilised in any form or by any electronic, mechanical, or other means, now known or hereafter invented, including photocopying and recording, or in any information storage or retrieval system, without permission in writing from the publishers.

Trademark notice: Product or corporate names may be trademarks or registered trademarks, and are used only for identification and explanation without intent to infringe.

British Library Cataloguing-in-Publication Data
A catalogue record for this book is available from the British Library

Library of Congress Cataloging-in-Publication Data
Names: Coyne, Richard, author.
Title: Peirce for architects / Richard Coyne.
Description: New York : Routledge, 2019. |
Series: Thinkers for architects | Includes bibliographical references and index.
Identifiers: LCCN 2018051773 (print) | LCCN 2018052502 (ebook) |
ISBN 9780429453816 (eBook) | ISBN 9781138319578 (hardback) |
ISBN 9781138319585 (pbk.)
Subjects: LCSH: Peirce, Charles S. (Charles Sanders), 1839–1914. |
Architecture–Philosophy.
Classification: LCC B945.P44 (ebook) |
LCC B945.P44 C69 2019 (print) | DDC 191–dc23
LC record available at https://lccn.loc.gov/2018051773

ISBN: 978-1-138-31957-8 (hbk)
ISBN: 978-1-138-31958-5 (pbk)
ISBN: 978-0-429-45381-6 (ebk)

Typeset in Frutiger
by Newgen Publishing UK

To Valerie

Contents

Series editor's preface   ix
List of figures and tables   xi
Acknowledgements   xiii

1. Introduction   1

    Outline of the book 6

2. Signs   10

    The tree and the weathervane 12
    Peirce's theory of signs 20
    Icons in architecture 23

3. Sign-Vehicles   29

    Icon 31
    Index 33
    Symbol 36
    Ten classes of signs 37
    First, Second, Third 41
    Breaking the rules 48
    The number three 52

4. Indexical architecture   58

    A return to the physical 58
    Signs and facts 61

      Translating indexical signs to symbols 64
      Diagrammatic proof 67

5. Abduction in architecture   70

      Abduction in the smart city 74
      Forensic architecture 76
      Indefinite inference 80
      Design as abduction 83
      Abduction versus interpretation 87

6. Nature semiotics   90

      Nature's signs 91
      Pansemiotics 94
      Geosemiotics 96
      The posthuman and speculative realism 98

7. Pragmatism   101

      Pragmatism and positivism 103
      Verification 106
      The power of practice 108
      Radicalising Peirce 110

Glossary	114
Further reading	118
References	120
Index	131

Series editor's preface

Adam Sharr

Architects have often looked to thinkers in philosophy and theory for design ideas, or in search of a critical framework for practice. Yet architects and students of architecture can struggle to navigate thinkers' writings. It can be daunting to approach original texts with little appreciation of their contexts. And existing introductions seldom explore a thinker's architectural material in any detail. This original series offers clear, quick and accurate introductions to key thinkers who have written about architecture. Each book summarises what a thinker has to offer for architects. It locates their architectural thinking in the body of their work, introduces significant books and essays, helps decode terms and provides quick reference for further reading. If you find philosophical and theoretical writing about architecture difficult, or just don't know where to begin, this series will be indispensable.

Books in the *Thinkers for Architects* series come out of architecture. They pursue architectural modes of understanding, aiming to introduce a thinker to an architectural audience. Each thinker has a unique and distinctive ethos, and the structure of each book derives from the character at its focus. The thinkers explored are prodigious writers and any short introduction can only address a fraction of their work. Each author – an architect or an architectural critic – has focused on a selection of a thinker's writings which they judge most relevant to designers and interpreters of architecture. Inevitably, much will be left out.

These books will be the first point of reference, rather than the last word, about a particular thinker for architects. It is hoped that they will encourage you to read further, offering an incentive to delve deeper into the original writings of a particular thinker.

The *Thinkers for Architects* series has proved highly successful, expanding to 14 volumes dealing with familiar cultural figures whose writings have influenced architectural designers, critics and commentators in distinctive and important ways. Books explore the work of: Gilles Deleuze and Felix Guattari; Martin Heidegger; Luce Irigaray; Homi Bhabha; Pierre Bourdieu; Walter Benjamin; Jacques Derrida; Hans-Georg Gadamer, Michael Foucault, Nelson Goodman, Henri Lefebvre, Paul Virilio, Maurice Merleau-Ponty, Immanuel Kant, and now Charles Sanders Peirce. The series continues to expand, addressing an increasingly rich diversity of thinkers who have something to say to architects.

Adam Sharr is Head of the School of Architecture, Planning and Landscape at Newcastle University, Principal of Adam Sharr Architects and Editor-in-Chief of *arq: Architectural Research Quarterly*, a Cambridge University Press international architecture journal. His books published by Routledge include *Heidegger for Architects* and *Reading Architecture and Culture*.

List of figures and tables

Figures

2. Signs
    1. Weathervane. Long Leg Gate Tower, Tallinn, Estonia. 13
    2. Saussure's depictions of the signified/signifier relationship, after Saussure. 14
    3. Reconstruction of an Iron Age Roundhouse at Llynnon Mill, Anglesey, Wales. 16
    4. Sketch (iconic sign) of the Taj Mahal. 22
    5. Iconic architecture. Dundee V&A by Kengo Kuma and Associates. 24

3. Sign-Vehicles
    6. Typological portico plan diagrams, after Durand. 32
    7. Derivation of Peirce's sign classifications: 27 combinations of 3x3 descriptors reduced to ten on the basis of his theory of dependencies between Firstness, Secondness and Thirdness. 47
    8. Peirce's sign classifications and their interdependencies. 49
    9. A single and a double tetractys. 53
    10. Ogden and Richard's semiotic triangle, after Ogden and Richards 56

4. Indexical architecture
    11. Pointing as an indexical sign. 60
    12. Smoke as an index of fire. Edinburgh Beltane Fire Festival. 67
    13. Peirce's simple diagrammatic proof that the two angles formed by a line that joins another along its length add up to two right angles. 68

5 Abduction in architecture

    14. A simple Venn diagram illustrating the syllogism. 72
    15. Evidence of an urban catastrophe. 79
    16. Permutations of the elements of the syllogism, after March. 85
    17. The three conditions and their relationships from which the circular segments in March's diagram are derived. 86

6. Nature semiotics

    18. Organic architecture. Reykjavík, Iceland. Harpa Concert Hall and Conference Centre, Henning Larsen Architects. 92
    19. Simulated fossilised organic entities by Asad Khan and Patricia Wu Wu. 93
    20. Evidence of geological sign processes, Rangárþing ytra, Suðurland, Iceland. 97

Tables

    1. Summary of Peirce's main classification of signs. 40
    2. Components of the sign situation and how they relate to Peirce's nine sign descriptors. 42
    3. Simplification of Table 3.2. 45

Acknowledgements

A PhD thesis by Dave Wood renewed my interest in C.S. Peirce. Jon Awbrey has been a consistent web correspondent on Peirce during this journey. Kamini Vellodi provided insights into Peirce and Deleuze on diagrams and commented on an early draft. Asad Khan provided information about contemporary philosophical theories and contemporary art practice. Graham Shawcross knows about diagrams, and Roxana Karam explores biosemiotics. Both are vigilant monitors of my online reflections that led to this book. Adam Sharr helped with clarity and consistency in the text. As ever I am grateful for the guidance of Adrian Snodgrass who introduced me to hermeneutics, a discipline that helps me make sense of any thinker for architects.

CHAPTER 1

Introduction

Few would deny that architecture communicates, and in that sense, *is* a language, or at least is *like* a language. The thinking of Charles Sanders Peirce (1839–1914) is of interest to architects mainly because of his contribution to how architecture operates as a language. Peirce's thinking is not as well known to architecture as that of the Swiss linguist Ferdinand de Saussure (1857–1913). In the hands of art, design, architecture and literary theorists, Saussure's ideas initiated the movements known as Structuralism and Poststructuralism. As we progress through Peirce's ideas I will make clear the differences between the legacies of Peirce and Saussure.

Peirce's contribution comes under the heading of *semiotics*, the theory of signs. He contributes to architecture in three ways to be explored in this book. The *first* is the language discussion to which I've already alluded, specifically his theory of signs. The *second* contribution from Peirce is in the nature of evidential reasoning, that is, reasoning from evidence. Peirce was a great systematiser and organiser of ideas. In fact, he considered himself a logician before he was a philosopher, a logician being someone who resorts to mathematics and formal symbolic systems to study the way people construct arguments and reach conclusions. In Peirce's words, 'Logic is the art of reasoning' (Peirce 1998f: 11). There is much in Peirce that appealed to twentieth-century systematisers in architecture. So, Peirce speaks to mathematicians, logicians, those systems theorists who seek orderly methods for solving the world's problems, and those of the Design Methods Movement (Langrish 2016) who seek orderly, mathematical and logical procedures for designing buildings. Peirce's influence extends to digital practitioners and programmers in architecture, and more recently those interested in big data, and responsive architecture that copies biological processes and forms (biomimesis). Peirce speaks to proponents of smart cities, as well as sustainable cities that cope with the challenges of a world in which human intervention has taken on the scale of geological processes – in the age of the Anthropocene. Peirce also speaks to those who conduct digitally enabled forensic analysis of places and spaces. Mathematician and pioneer of computer-aided architecture Lionel March introduced his edited book *The Architecture of Form* with an examination of Peirce's concepts of induction, deduction and abduction (March 1976). It turns out that Peirce's ideas about logic demonstrate the limits of logic, but also suggest how ideas from formal logic can be recruited in design, and here Peirce's thinking interacts with theories about the interpretation of places and buildings, that is, Hermeneutics and Phenomenology (Snodgrass and Coyne 2006; Kidder 2013).

The *third* contribution of Peirce is his pragmatism. Most philosophers have delegated Peirce as the leading figure in the philosophical school that bears that name. This school of Pragmatism positions itself against any notion, as Rene Descartes seemed to propose, that thought is an abstract activity divorced from the everyday lifeworld. Ideas from Pragmatism resonate with Phenomenology and some of Martin Heidegger's (Sharr 2007) and Merleau-Ponty's (Hale 2016) thinking. Architecture is a practical and pragmatic discipline, and a study of Peirce emphasises architecture as a practice, and a practice grounded in the materiality of the world. Unlike other thinkers headlined in the *Thinkers for Architecture* series, there is no Peircean architecture as such, and no particular movement, style or body of work that demonstrates allegiance to him. But in so far as any practitioner, educator or critic claims to be *pragmatic*, they owe a debt, however indirectly, to Peirce's thinking.

Architecture is a practical and pragmatic discipline, and a study of Peirce emphasises architecture as a practice, and a practice grounded in the materiality of the world.

An interesting thread works through each of these three aspects of Peirce's thinking, and that is the notion of *indexicality*. Peirce begins his sign theory with three basic classes of signs: icon, index and symbol. As I will show in the rest of this book, the idea of the index is crucial to Peirce, and impinges on his concepts of creative reasoning, as well as his pragmatism. An indexical sign is an item of evidence grounded in actual material observation. The indexical is at the heart of Peirce's sign system, is present in his argument about abductive reasoning, and supports his orientation to the tangible world of practical engagement. If I were to attach a label to Peirce's contribution to our field I would call it 'indexical architecture'.

<u>the idea of the index is crucial to Peirce, and impinges on his concepts of creative reasoning, as well as his pragmatism.</u>

For explicit evidence of the connections between Peirce's semiotics and architecture we need look no further than the important book from 1969 entitled *Meaning in Architecture*, edited by Charles Jencks and George Baird (1969), and in particular the contributions in that book by Geoffrey Broadbent (1969). Other architectural theorists had investigated the language theme, but that book in particular brings the mainstream of architectural thinking into contact with Peirce. Another book of which Broadbent was a co-editor and contributor followed ten years later, *Signs, Symbols, and Architecture* (Broadbent et al. 1980). Though he seemed to start with Peirce, Broadbent later veered towards a critical engagement with Structuralism, and he co-wrote a book published in 1991 on Deconstruction (Broadbent and Glusberg 1991), and hence the influence of Jacques Derrida on architecture (Coyne 2011). Another advocate of Peircean semiotics is the philosopher and literary theorist Umberto Eco (1932–2016). Though he is more closely aligned with literature, Eco has a chapter in *Signs, Symbols, and Architecture* (Eco 1980). Another publication of note is that of the art historian Donald Preziosi who wrote *Architecture, Language and Meaning: Origins of the Built World and Its Semiotic Organization* (Preziosi 1979), a book that draws substantially on Peirce. Peirce is there in architectural conversations, though not always in the foreground.

I think a supplementary contribution Peirce makes to architecture is in the art of his geometrical constructions. Though his work lacks compelling diagrams that might appeal to architects, he describes and illustrates various theories about the way signs work. If you are used to binaries and oppositional thinking, then Peirce provides a challenge. He was a philosopher of *threes*. There are three components to the logical syllogism, three parts to any sign situations, three types of signs, three terms defining each sign category, and sign types come in the shape of a pyramid. This is triadic thinking. He referred to his own obsession as *triadomany*, and others have even referred to his style as *triadomania* (Spinks 1991). I think there is an intriguing aesthetic dimension to Peirce's work that should appeal to any architect interested in the *shape* that ideas take.

Considering the case I have been making about his relevance to architecture, you may ask what Peirce ever wrote about the subject of architecture, or space, place, cities and environments. The short answer is 'very little'. His insight is about process rather than product. As with much philosophy, it is left to others to apply those methods in their domain of interest. In an essay with the promising title *The Architecture of Theories*, Peirce outlines the 'power of thinking' someone has to exercise before constructing a house, involving the complex task of selecting available and suitable materials, deciding the best mode of construction and 'a hundred such questions'. Learning from the metaphor of building, he said: 'the studies preliminary to the construction of a great theory should be at least as deliberate and thorough as those that are preliminary to the building of a dwelling-house' (Peirce 1992b: 286). The *architecture* in the title of the essay refers in fact to the ubiquity of *three*: 'the conceptions of First, Second, Third' (1992b: 296) that according to Peirce underpin philosophy, psychology and biology. In basic terms, there is (First) a thing that exists independently of anything else, (Second) the relationships between such independent things, and (Third) the mediation by which Firsts and Seconds are brought into relationship. This again is Peirce's triadic thinking theme. In this essay, he does not bring triadic thinking back to the dwelling house with which he begins. It would be up to architects to explore how triadic architectural motifs such as *firmitas*, *commoditas* and *venustas* (firmness, commodity and delight) (Vitruvius 1960) relate to Peirce's structuring of thought.

It is fair to say that Peirce's interests align more closely with the natural sciences than with fine art or architecture. He did much of his writing whilst working for the U.S. Coast and Geodetic Survey, which involved surveying and measuring variations in the intensity of the Earth's gravitational field. So, he was closely connected with geology, earth science, mathematics and engineering, and he was trained as a chemist. His ideas about signs have been taken up by philosophers of science and biology to advance a theory of *biosemiotics* (Sebeok 1999), and *geosemiotics* by geologists who champion in particular the theme of the Anthropocene (Szerszynski 2017). I mention these threads as they pertain to environment, for which the connections with Peirce's life and work are easy to establish. I have explored these environmental themes more fully and with reference to Peirce in another book, *Network Nature* (Coyne 2018).

I have as yet hardly introduced Peirce the person. Philosopher Albert Atkin provides a recent and accessible account of Peirce's life and ideas (Atkin 2016), and the online *Stanford Encyclopedia of Philosophy* provides a further authoritative account that is within easy reach of any scholar (Burch 2017). From these accounts, we learn that Peirce was a prodigious writer, with a career spanning 57 years, during which time he published about 12,000 printed pages and about 80,000 unpublished handwritten pages. By way of comparison, little survives of Saussure's writing, except what his students compiled from his lecture notes as a single book after his death (Saussure 1983). The most accessible collection of Peirce's work is provided as volumes one and two of *The Essential Peirce* published by Indiana University Press (Peirce 1992a, 1998a). It is worth noting that at the end of the nineteenth century not yet under the influence of rapid electronic communication, Peirce and Saussure were unaware of each other's work.

In spite of his Harvard education, a father who was a Professor of Mathematics at Harvard, and his own immense productivity, Peirce was unable to secure a tenured academic post. He taught for five years at Johns Hopkins University.

Amongst those he taught were Thorstein Veblen (Veblen 1998) and John Dewey (Dewey 1958), but he never rose to a position of comparable prominence or academic security. Peirce was often in financial difficulty, particularly after he divorced his first wife following an extra-marital affair that cost him his job at Johns Hopkins. Atkin said of Peirce that he 'was, by all accounts, an awkward and irascible man' but adds that he 'nonetheless inspired considerable affection and devotion in those close to him' (Atkin 2016: 1). One of Peirce's closest allies was the philosopher and psychologist William James (1842–1910) who promoted Peirce as the founder of Pragmatism and provided opportunities for Peirce's ideas to circulate. He also provided Peirce with some financial support.

Peirce's thinking provides an excellent foil against which to test ideas important to architecture. Though he was a child of the nineteenth century, his thinking anticipates some progressive and controversial thinking emerging in the twenty-first century relevant to architecture, including a renewed appreciation of what makes places significant and liveable.

> Though he was a child of the nineteenth century, his thinking anticipates some progressive and controversial thinking emerging in the twenty-first century relevant to architecture, including a renewed appreciation of what makes places significant and liveable.

Outline of the book

I follow Peirce's ideas, starting with his most conspicuous contribution to architecture, namely his theories of signs, and progress via his concepts of the indexical sign to his theories of evidence and inference. I then consider his so-called pansemiotics and naturalism, before summarising his thinking under the heading of *pragmatism*. Each chapter builds on the previous chapter to construct a picture of Peirce's impact on architectural thinking.

After this introduction, I present in the second chapter, *Signs*, Peirce's three sign classifications: icon, index and symbol, and how these have been taken up in architecture. Peirce's theory of signs represented an alternative strand to the Structuralist discourse popular within architecture in the 1960s and 1970s. Peirce put semiotics on a different footing to his contemporary Saussure. As a logician, Peirce was concerned with the way we formulate and transform logical statements, which are made up of signs. Peirce is best known within art, design and architecture for his contribution to semiotics. He proposed a taxonomy of signs, which includes the icon, the index and the symbol, with other categories within these. I provide architectural examples of each of these categories and subcategories, but also observe how these terms have circulated as part of the common currency of architecture, even without recourse to Peirce's intricate taxonomy.

In Chapter 3 on *Sign-vehicles*, I explore Peirce's complex theory of signs in full. He defined three elements of the sign: the sign-vehicle, the object and the interpretant. He constructed his three main sign classifications within this triadic structure, which he in turn explored in terms of three further categories that he interfaced with the concepts of First, Second and Third. But Peirce also elaborated on the nature of that component of a sign situation that delivers the sign: the sign-vehicle. In this schema he incorporated notions of quality, the immediacy and directness of a sign, whether or not it is articulated in language, its credibility as part of a convention, rule or law, and its place in the world of facts and logic. Peirce developed his theories over time, but the most enduring is his ten classifications of signs arranged in a pyramidal diagram. I explain each of his sign concepts with reference to architecture.

In Chapter 4, *Indexical architecture*, I probe the important class of the indexical sign and its innovative role in Peirce's semiotics. I show how the logic of the index relates to the way signs appear as evidence, and hence Peirce's characterisation of what he called *abductive* inference. I posit an indexical architecture as one that is grounded, embodied and responsive.

In Chapter 5 on *Abduction in architecture*, I address the issues of evidence, and its relationship with the indexical sign. Within the logical, Peircean frame it is helpful to think of design as a translation from one set of signs, or propositions, to another set of signs, that is, as *inference*. Peirce highlights different modes of inference. His innovative thinking about different types of reasoning and inference holds sway in some quarters, in particular his idea of *abductive*, or evidential, reasoning developed in architecture by Lionel March and others, working with formal systems and computers. Peirce used the term 'interpretant' to mean the effect of a sign on the person who understands it. In this chapter, I tackle the relationship between Peirce's concepts of interpretation and those advanced by phenomenological philosophers such as Martin Heidegger and Hans-Georg Gadamer.

Chapter 6 is about *Nature semiotics*. Peirce's semiotics is translated into biosemiotics and geosemiotics by followers of Peirce, themes relevant to biomimetic architecture, landscape architecture, sustainability and environment. An important implication of Peirce's philosophy is that semiotic, communicative structures already exist within the natural world, and between human beings and the world, themes developed further by the biologist Thomas Sebeok, and for whom a biosemiotics has currency. In this chapter, I touch on Peirce's anticipation of what is now called *posthumanism* and an orientation to environment that speculates on what the world would be like in the absence of human beings (so-called *speculative realism*).

In Chapter 7, I draw attention to more recent philosophers aligned with Pragmatism such as Richard Rorty, who, at the height of the postmodern turn, drew these various discourses together. Some architectural theorists interested in Pragmatism have been attracted to Peirce, who provides a framework for situating some of the more positivist discourses in architecture from the 1960s and 1970s, in particular the Design Methods Movement. I conclude by drawing together the threads of the book and summarising the case for Peirce as a radical contributor to architectural thinking. A study of Peirce provides an opportunity to unpack the relationships between important philosophical and theoretical movements, including Logical Positivism, Phenomenology, Structuralism, Poststructuralism and Pragmatism, as well as critical and radical philosophies of knowledge.

Peirce introduces many terms that may challenge the reader. I will avoid airing the confusion I share with many others on the distinctions between semiotics and semiosis, or debates about 'pragmatism' and 'pragmaticism', or showing how his ideas developed and changed throughout his career. Even the pronunciation of Peirce's name provides a stumbling block for students of his work, until we note its peculiar spelling, and habituate ourselves to pronouncing the name as 'purse' instead of 'pierce'. When it comes to the importance of the term 'index' in Peirce's lexicon, I will avoid the correct but unfamiliar term 'indices' to indicate its plural, and where possible will refer to 'indexical signs' or simply 'indexicals'. 'Indexical' serves as a noun or adjective. To the best of my knowledge, Peirce does not use the term 'indexicality', but others do, and I will adopt it where appropriate. I have summarised some of Peirce's key terms and those within semiotics in a short glossary at the end of the book.

CHAPTER 2

Signs

Peirce's most important contribution to architecture and the arts, as well as digital interaction design (De Souza and Barbosa 2006; Wood 2016) is his theory of signs, semiotics. According to Alfred Nöth's extensive *Handbook of Semiotics*, the story of semiotics spans from Plato (428 BC–348 BC) to the twentieth century (Nöth 1990). Ancient and religious literature often referred to signs, symbols, symptoms and naming, but semiotics as a study only came to light as scholars began to discuss and debate such ideas. For example, Plato expressed his suspicion of signs (which he referred to as 'names'). He said about things that exist 'it is far better to investigate them and learn about them through themselves than to do so through their names' (Plato 1997: 154). Aristotle, and ancient philosophers such as the Stoics and the Epicureans, continued to debate the role of signs in the relationship between the human and the world.

Peirce's most important contribution to architecture and the arts, is his theory of signs, semiotics.

The first mention of semiotics as a study in philosophy came with John Locke's (1632–1704) *Essay Concerning Human Understanding*, in which Locke outlines a *doctrine of signs* (Locke 1976). He thought 'ideas and words' are 'the great instruments of knowledge' (1976: 443). But, according to Nöth it was the mathematicians Johann Heinrich Lambert (1728–1777) and Bernard Bolzano (1781–1848) who later gave the theory of signs a systematic treatment. Most scholars think of their successor, Peirce, as the first serious exponent of a theory of signs. He wrote extensively on the subject.

But Peirce's theories about signs are not the most widely adopted amongst architectural scholars. Architects may be more familiar with theories linking architecture to signs through Structuralism, a movement in philosophy, psychology, linguistics and the arts that identifies the structures underlying everyday phenomena. Many of us working in architecture and the arts are exposed to Structuralism via the work of the Swiss linguist Ferdinand de Saussure (1857–1913) (Saussure 1983; Hawkes 2003) and his followers. Saussure's ideas were disseminated only posthumously, as his students documented the contents of his lectures and compiled them into the book *Course in General Linguistics* (Saussure 1983). Saussure left no writings of his own. Peirce on the other hand was well known as a philosopher, a discipline with wider reach than Saussure's field of linguistics. Even though he was never a career academic, Peirce's work achieved wide recognition in his lifetime.

Though they did not know of each other's work, both scholars were of course aware of the history of their disciplines. Saussure referenced this sketchily in a chapter 'A Brief Survey of the History of Linguistics'. But as a philosopher, Peirce drew on the legacies of Kant, Hegel, the Romantics, John Locke, Charles Darwin and a wide array of sources throughout his career. Peirce was familiar with traditions of thinking about the sign, as well as the many other themes he addressed in his writing. Peirce was well positioned in the established canon of European and American thought, and yet Saussure was the one who became more influential in architecture, indirectly and through his followers.

As I stated in Chapter 1, the main text that brought to light semiotics, Structuralism and language in architecture, at least in the anglophone tradition, was the seminal 1969 book *Meaning in Architecture* (Jencks and Baird 1969). The book makes copious reference to Saussure but mentions Peirce in only one section. In his chapter, 'Meaning into architecture', architectural scholar, Broadbent wrote, 'The relationship between words and the thing they stand for was first investigated systematically by the American philosopher, Charles Sanders Peirce (1838–1914)' (Broadbent 1969: 53).

Broadbent then goes on to explain some differences in terminology deployed by Peirce and Saussure: 'He called this science of signs "semiotic" and it is typical of the confusion in this field that the Saussureans now call it "semiology" ' (1969: 53). In what follows I will dispense with such distinctions and use the term 'semiotics' throughout. But the differences between Saussure and Peirce are more than terminological.

Meaning in Architecture was followed 11 years later by a publication from the same community of scholars, the 1980 book *Signs, Symbols and Architecture* (Broadbent et al. 1980). By then, Peirce's writings had greater traction in the English-speaking architectural canon. That book includes two key chapters drawing on Peirce, one by the philosopher Umberto Eco (1980), the other by Broadbent (1980) who co-edited the volume. Broadbent had published a book in 1973 about design methods, called *Design in Architecture: Architecture and the Human Sciences* (Broadbent 1973). That book laid out diverse approaches to design, including its putative automation by computer, as well as an explanation of Saussure's concepts of the sign. The book also included what Broadbent regarded as his main contribution at the time, an explanation of four approaches to design: pragmatic, iconic, analogic and canonic. In *Signs, Symbols and Architecture* he aligned these classes to Peirce's three classifications of the sign: icon, index and symbol (Broadbent 1980). I think of Broadbent as one of the major scholars who brought Peirce to architecture, not least as his investigations spanned from a computational orientation to one grounded more in philosophy and the humanities, a trajectory similar to the spectrum of Peirce's work.

The tree and the weathervane

As a simple introduction to the two thinkers (Saussure and Peirce), consider the examples on which they draw to illustrate the operations of the sign. They both use many examples, but one stands out in the case of each author. Saussure illustrates how a sign works by showing how the word 'tree' refers to the concept of a tree, and he provides a simple diagram of a lone tree standing

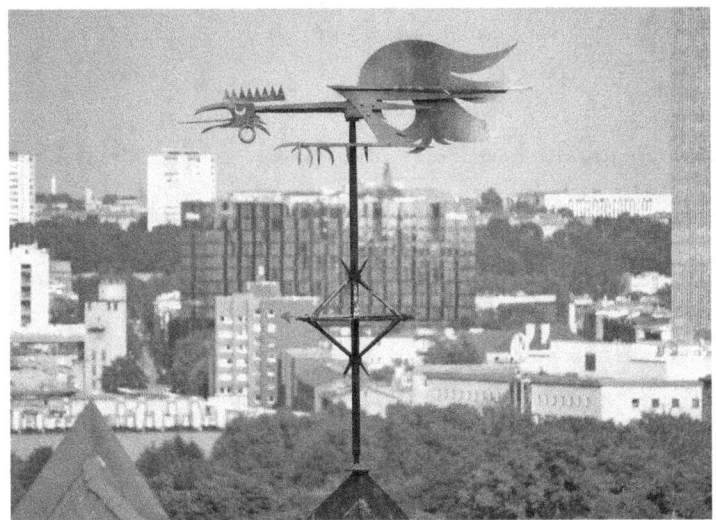

Figure 1 Weathervane. Long Leg Gate Tower, Tallinn, Estonia.
Source: Author.

in a field. On the other hand, Peirce illustrates the working of the sign with a weathervane on the top of a building. The orientation of this mechanism serves as a sign indicating the direction of the wind. Of note, the tree as a whole features in Saussure's illustrations; the weathervane has functioning parts. The tree is a concept to which a sign refers; the vane functions as a sign. In what follows, I will show the differences that these emblematic examples bring to light. As a further rule of thumb to help navigate the differences between Saussure and Peirce, think of Structuralism as a philosophy of *twos*, that is, binaries and oppositions. As I will show later, Peirce's is a philosophy of *threes*, and he makes much of the significance of the number three.

Saussure provided several innovations to thinking that have resonated throughout the twentieth century. It is worth reviewing these briefly before examining Peirce's contribution, which follows a different path. As Saussure showed, it is simple enough to think of language as based on two components: the word, and the thing to which the word refers. A word (such

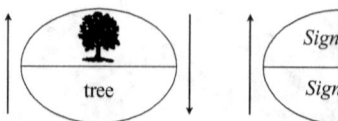

Figure 2 Saussure's depictions of the signified/signifier relationship, after Saussure (1983: 67).
Source: Author.

as *tree*) is easier to manipulate, reason about and transmit to other people than an actual tree, the thing that the word references. As the philosopher John Locke observed (1632–1704), things in themselves are not present to the mind for contemplation unless we use signs: 'to communicate our thoughts to one another, as well as record them for our own use, signs of our ideas are also necessary' (Locke 1976: 443). As well as spoken and written words, language may be made up of symbols, hieroglyphics and images. To generalise this linguistic economy further, Saussure spoke of *the signifier* (rather than *the word*), and *the thing* to which it refers as *the signified*. That is the first major binary of Structuralism, sometimes expressed as the signified/signifier relationship, the combination of which constitutes a *sign situation*.

We do not need to restrict the signified to an actual, specific tree, but the idea of a tree. To make the distinction even more abstract, Saussure also referred to a sign as a link between a sound image and a concept. Many commentators point out that there is already something radical in Saussure's formulation of the sign, and that opens language to its possibility beyond a mere vehicle for describing what is in the world (Hawkes 2003). As well as tangible objects, it is obvious that the *signified* can also be an idea or a concept. Less obviously, the signified can also be another signifier. Language has this fluidity, to the extent that we use words without requiring that they settle on anything tangible or 'real'.

Structuralism has this interesting by-product whereby it dispenses with the need to scrutinise a reality outside of language. Structuralism focuses on words and concepts, and their relationships, rather than an independent reality to which those words might refer. Saussure identified the non-semiotic world, a world outside of what we say about it, as 'a vague, uncharted nebula' (Saussure 1996: 99). He also said, 'nothing is distinct before the appearance of language' (1996: 99). Nöth described Saussure's position as 'transsemiotic agnosticism', which is to assert 'nothing can be said about the non semiotic world' (Nöth 1990: 81). So, according to Saussure, we cannot say anything about the world other than what is exercised by and between human beings and their cultural systems. Saussure's semiotics is therefore *anthropocentric*, that is, human centred, depending on human language and culture. Critics argue against Structuralism as it sometimes presents language and hence knowledge as social and conventional, with no grounding in concepts of a concrete reality, or a real world, outside of language. In summary, Structuralism's first binary is between the signifier and the signified, and subsumes, excludes or diminishes the tangible, the material and the concrete in that formulation.

Structuralism has this interesting by-product whereby it dispenses with the need to scrutinise a reality outside of language.

A second binary feature of Structuralism relates to meaning. Conventionally, we might think that the meaning of a word is what it corresponds to, in the case of a tree, the tree in the field, trees in general, or the concept of a tree. Again, a Structuralist does not think that a sentence is meaningful because it references the tangible things of the world. According to Saussure, meaning resides in *difference* – and the differences between sounds: 'The sound of a word is not in itself important, but the phonetic contrasts which allow us to distinguish that word from any other. That is what carries the meaning' (Saussure 1983: 116).

Saussure's key text on language is populated with linguistic examples, including illustrations of words that sound similar and their phonemic subtleties within

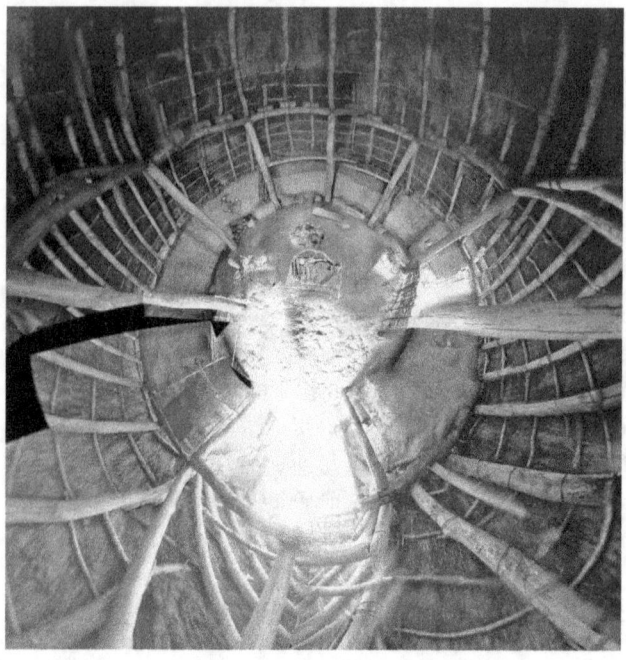

Figure 3 Reconstruction of an Iron Age Roundhouse at Llynnon Mill, Anglesey, Wales.
Source: Author.

and across different languages. Architectural scholars are likely to be less interested in such linguistic details, but certain theorists have extended the notion of difference into other aspects of culture. The anthropologist Claude Lévi-Strauss (1908–2009) established binary opposition and difference as the main components in a Structuralist understanding of culture (Lévi-Strauss 1963). For example, anthropologists following a Structuralist strategy might identify various oppositions within the organisation of a traditional village, for example, how raw produce is kept separate from cooked food in the way the village is arranged spatially, or how there are parts of the village organised in terms of gender (male and female), or the village may consist of lodges organised according to animal species (bears versus eagles). Structuralism presents a world permeated by such binaries.

The third main binary feature of language to which Saussure alludes assumes there are two tiers to any sign situation. There is the surface phenomenon and the deep structure of a language situation. At the surface, you have the particularities of any dialect or language (French, English, Chinese), including individual peculiarities of speech, accent and the use of idioms. On the other hand, the deep structure refers to what the speaker says, independently of the apparent surface expression. In Saussure's terms, and deploying common terms in French, at the surface you have what he calls *parole*, the way things are spoken; whereas the deep structure is the *langue*, the basic tongue or language of the community. Following a science model, at least in its origins, Structuralism sought to generalise across a range of diverse phenomena, which meant identifying the deep structures (*langue*). Building on Saussure's work, Lévi-Strauss observed the kinds of oppositions you might find in any community: raw versus cooked, male versus female, bears versus eagles. That is the *parole*. But beneath the surface reside binary structures that are common to a range of observations across many different cultural phenomena. He employed the notion of *bricolage* to account for the surface phenomenon, the *parole*. We human beings adopt whatever is to hand, he argued, to give expression to deep and underlying binary differences. Many of the *parole* phenomena Lévi-Strauss observed in different countries were products of local particularities, evident not least in climatic conditions and the availability of animal species with which to articulate differences: bears and eagles in one region, but snakes and buzzards in another. This formulation further deflects from a concern with the everyday lifeworld and its materiality. Local, worldly phenomena are understood here as surface features, beneath which reside the more important structures that provide unity across different phenomena.

The main challenge of a Structuralist analysis resides in identifying these deep structures: the *langue*, to which the *parole* gives expression. For some theorists, Lévi-Strauss amongst them, there is a psychological, or psychoanalytic, substrate to human organisation, something like Sigmund Freud's (1856–1939) account of the human psyche in terms of conflicts about our relationships as infants with our parents, the loss of intimacy with our mothers, and how such conflicts get re-enacted, reinforced or resolved as we pass through key stages in our lives (Freud 1991). Cultural theorists such as Roland Barthes (1915–1980) followed a critique closely aligned with Karl Marx (1818–1883), implicating class differences and the way one group dominates another (Barthes 1973). The message of Structuralism is that we need to be suspicious of any messaging, particularly in the mass media, and advertising that conceals hidden communications, and that seeks to reinforce established power structures and establish or re-establish class domination.

In fact, some commentators (Ricoeur 1977) identify an affinity between Freudian psychoanalysis, Neo-Marxism and Structuralism. Each is concerned with uncovering what lies beneath the surface. For Structuralism it is the *langue*, that is, some deeper meaning structure, for Freud it is the unconscious, and for the neo-Marxists it is hegemony (the domination of one class over another). Through these affinities, whether or not by avowed adherence, Structuralism provides a framework that supports various critical, social and political agendas in architecture. It also provides an entry point for reviewing traditional architectural theories, many of which present themselves in oppositional terms: such as form and function, structure and ornament, global and local, the divine and the secular, nature and culture, and the literal and the metaphorical.

The Structuralism in architecture of the 1970s transformed into what was called Poststructuralism, particularly under the influence of the philosopher Jacques Derrida (1930–2004) (Derrida 1986), whose impact I address in *Derrida for Architects* (Coyne 2011). Derrida adapted Saussure's initial characterisation of the loose relationship between the signifier and the signified to argue that signifiers typically refer to other signifiers in endless chains of signification. Meaning resides in the trace through such chains, and meaning is difficult to pin down. He also showed that in identifying oppositions, we need to pay regard to the implied superiority, or dominance, of one term over the other. We often think of words and their opposites: freedom versus restraint, listening versus seeing, writing versus speaking, whole versus fragmented. We accord one term greater importance than the other. One term defines the other: for example, freedom is superior to restraint, and restraint is defined as a lack of freedom. For Derrida, such oppositions are not evenly balanced. Nor is the priority that we assume always the case. For example, every attempt we make to define freedom, assumes some starting point in a concept of restraint. Structuralism's appeal to deep structures implies some eventual certainty to our understanding, as long as we can find it. For Poststructuralists such certainties are elusive; the ground of our certainties is at best shaky.

In summary, I think of the legacies of Structuralism and Poststructuralism in architecture as modes of analysis that foreground the critical, social and political. We can also think about what Structuralism leaves out. In spite of its claim to access underlying structures, it stops short of identifying detailed classifications or typologies as aids to decision-making, design or thought in general. Structuralists do not suggest methods for designing so much as frameworks for critique. The architects Aldo van Eyck (1918–1999) and Herman Hertzberger (b. 1932) associated their work strongly with Structuralism. They were also involved in an organisation known as Team 10 that sought to break away from abstract modernism and claimed to restore a sense of meaning, place, context and humanity in its buildings (Risselada and van den Heuvel 2005). Structuralism foregrounded the issues of *meaning* in architecture, but the application of the ideas within Structuralism reaches further than any group of buildings or group of practising architects.

I think of the legacies of Structuralism and Poststructuralism in architecture as modes of analysis that foreground the critical, social and political.

Structuralism claims extremely wide applicability. Lévi-Strauss introduced Structuralism to anthropology, and Jean Piaget introduced it to psychology. Roland Barthes applied Structuralist analysis to a wide range of cultural phenomena: paintings, posters, food, drink, fashion and social practices (Barthes 1973). There was a strong political dimension to Barthes' cultural analysis. The Structuralist approach of analysis is applicable to any text (a street sign, newspaper headline, report, legal contract, script or great literary work), and any kind of building (shed, speculative housing scheme, office block, iconic building, or a whole city).

For some scholars, the discourse of Structuralism provided justification for an architecture that emphasised meaning, ahead of supposed detached modernist functionality, support for the view that architecture communicates, and that the ostensibly functional is not always as it seems. Of course, there are other discourses addressed in the *Thinkers for Architects* series, on which architectural scholars draw and that I shall say more about later in this book, notably studies in Phenomenology, Posthumanism, and gender and post-colonial studies (Rawes 2007; Hernández 2010), as well as emerging areas such as speculative realism (Meillassoux 2009).

I have focused so far on Structuralism as it is the loudest voice amongst those who look to language to understand architecture. Nöth's expansive *Handbook of Semiotics* with which I began this chapter is of particular note. It falls outside the orbit of mainstream architectural scholarship, in part due to the timing of its publication. By 1990 the appetite for elaborating on semiotics had waned as an impetus for architectural scholarship, and the *Handbook* makes no gestures towards architecture as an independent or heroic discipline above others. The book includes the application of semiotic theories to the sciences, art, music and architecture. In the case of the latter it references the work of several German scholars whose work did not make it into the English-speaking architectural canon, and I shall reference these later, for example, Elisabeth Walther.

Peirce's theory of signs

As a simple introduction to Peirce's contribution to semiotics, it is worth starting with his basic classification of signs (or what Saussure would have called *signifiers*). Those of us attuned to some of the subtleties of Poststructuralism, Phenomenology and neo-Marxism might think of classification as a low order of scholarship, analogous to nineteenth-century encyclopaedism, the attempt to comprehensively summarise, tabulate and catalogue knowledge, as in an encyclopaedia. A classificatory approach to architecture reveals itself in the identification of building types – as if the end point of scholarly investigation is to define building types, and to identify the categories to which individual buildings belong: civic, religious, retail, industrial, domestic, etc. Considering his propensity to classify, Peirce's thinking offers appeal to scholars inclined towards system, order, computation and logic. After all Peirce was a logician. But as I will show, Peirce's classifications of the sign resonate with broader aspects of architecture, and aspects left out of a Structuralist account.

As an introduction to his approach to classification, consider Peirce's major conjecture that a sign can either be an *icon*, an *index*, or a *symbol*. In Peirce's own words, 'Signs are of three classes, namely *Icons* (or images), *Indices*, and *Symbols*' (Peirce 1998f: 13). An *icon* is a sign that resembles its object (referent or signified in Saussure's terminology) in some way. An obvious example would be a drawing of the Taj Mahal. The drawing is an iconic sign of the object it refers to. There is a physical resemblance. It 'looks like' the building. On the other hand, an *indexical* sign is one that has some inevitable link with the object to which it refers. It emanates from the object: a crack in the wall of the Taj Mahal is a sign indicating a disturbance in the foundations under the building. A crack in a wall is an indicator (or *index*) in a way that someone's sketch of the Taj Mahal is not. We might also think of an index as a *symptom* of the object it refers to. The third sign class is the *symbol*. According to some experts, the Taj Mahal is a symbol of Shah Jahan's love for his (favourite) wife. The building's form bears no iconic resemblance to that love, or the wife. Nor does the building emerge inevitably as if an index, or an inevitable consequence of that love. In fact, the symbolic relationship between the sign and the object to which it refers is only established through a complex understanding borne of social circumstances and social convention, and even dispute. That is the nature of the symbolic sign according to Peirce. It is decided by social convention.

As an introduction to his approach to classification, consider Peirce's major conjecture that a sign can either be an *icon*, an *index*, or a *symbol*.

Figure 4 Sketch (iconic sign) of the Taj Mahal.
Source: Author.

Already, the Structuralist might object to Peirce's schema, asserting with Saussure that all signs have the property Peirce ascribes to symbols. The relationship between the signifier and the signified is inevitably decided by convention. In Saussure's terms, it is 'arbitrary' (Saussure 1983: 67). A follower of Peirce would respond that the three sign classes make a distinction that has some pragmatic use, arguing that it is expedient to distinguish between icons, indices and symbols. After all, a sketch of a building, a crack in a wall and a building as a symbol of love are sufficiently different aspects of communication to warrant assignment to different classes.

A second objection is that these sign classes seem to have very fluid boundaries. A sketch of a building may function as an icon, but a photograph is both an icon, in that it resembles the object to which it refers, and an index, as it results from an automated process linking the object to its representation. As with any system of classification in the arts and sciences there are crossovers between classes, and other complications that require interpretation. In part, Peirce addresses these complications by developing a much more elaborate classification system than suggested by the simple triplet of icon, index and symbol. I will discuss his classes of signs in the next chapter.

A third objection to Peirce's system is that if you are going to start by dividing the semiotic sphere into three classes, you may as well start with more, or less, than three. In fact, the semiotic scholar and follower of Peirce, Thomas Sebeok proposed six sign classes: the signal, symptom, icon, index, symbol and name (Sebeok 1999). As we shall see, Peirce did not restrict his classification to three, but actually proposed ten sign classes, derived from the initial three, and not simply by forming subclasses. He later expanded his classifications to 66 (Peirce 1998g: 481)! The contemporary scholar might entertain the possibility that Peirce uses these classifications as a temporary scaffolding from which to launch a challenge to some other entrenched convention. Later, I will show to what extent Peirce's sign classifications serve as a provocation, or that they can be deployed as such by his followers. Before elaborating further on Peirce's sign system, I will review attempts to apply his basic icon-index-symbol schema to architecture.

Icons in architecture

In his 1973 book *Design in Architecture*, Broadbent outlined four types of design, alluding to the methods by which architecture is produced. Elsewhere in that book he wrote about semiotics, but without reference to Peirce. We may assume that Broadbent's classifications arose independently of Peirce's icon, index and symbol sign classes (Broadbent 1980). Broadbent approached the subject of design through the idea of the icon.

According to Peirce, and conventional wisdom, an icon is a likeness; something that resembles the thing it refers to – its object or referent. Iconography is a branch of study that deals with such resemblances, that is, drawings or other pictorial representations of things. In spite of such generality, we mostly reserve

Figure 5 Iconic architecture. Dundee V&A by Kengo Kuma and Associates. Source: Author.

the word *icon* for use in particular contexts, such as in religious art, where it usually points to the godhead and the saints, particularly where ritual is involved. We may also say that an icon is a significant representation, or at least a resemblance of something that is important. I think that is the main inheritance people draw on when describing a work of art or a building as iconic. The iconic object is at or near the top of a hierarchy of importance. The icon may also stand in for a class of objects, or it may represent that class.

an icon is a likeness; something that resembles the thing it refers to – its object or referent.

For something to be iconic it must stand out at least as a visual image. Architecture tends to promote that definition. Iconic buildings gain their status by being visually distinct (Jencks 2005). The Oxford English Dictionary (OED) supports that definition (as a 2001 addition) to the conventional idea of a pictorial representation: 'A person or thing regarded as a representative symbol, esp. of a culture or movement; a person, institution, etc., considered worthy of admiration or respect'.

Developers and users of digital media also adopted the word *icon* to identify a patch of pixels on a display screen. That is another convention that has emerged since the advent of high quality bitmap screen displays. In that context an icon is a small image connected to some function in computer code.

Returning to the theme of iconic architecture, buildings can be iconic, in so far as they are 'considered worthy of admiration or respect' (OED). But to design in an iconic way would be to simply copy such respected sources. This is the proposition advanced by Broadbent. He explained the process of iconic design as the case where a new design is simply a copy of a well-established and proven design resolution developed by others. He thought of this as the least sophisticated approach to designing. He said pejoratively in his later article 'Building Design as an Iconic Sign System', that this approach is 'still used by lesser architects in following the designs of the great "form-givers" ' (Broadbent 1980: 311). Miles Glendinning described iconic architecture similarly as 'the architecture of metaphoric excess' (Glendinning 2010: 36). It seems Iconic architecture is not always architecture 'considered worthy of admiration or respect' (OED), but it is architecture copied from that class.

Broadbent contrasted the iconic approach to design with *pragmatic* design, from which much iconic design derives. Pragmatic design emerges over time from circumstances best represented in Broadbent's account of vernacular architecture – buildings developed by trial and error and in response to local circumstances over many generations. Iconic design circumvents that pragmatic development simply by copying the results of such pragmatic designs.

Beyond iconic design Broadbent identified *analogical* design. Why copy the forms of other tried and tested pragmatically designed buildings? To design by analogy is to copy forms and solutions from other contexts, such as forms from botany or geology, as exemplified in biomimetic architecture (Gruber 2011).

His fourth classification was *canonic* design, which is to design following a system, such as a grid or other geometrical schema, evident throughout the history of building, but reaching its apogee with industrialisation and prefabrication. A canon is a rule or law, hence Broadbent's use of 'canonic' to describe this latter process. Following Structuralist terminology, this design method draws on 'deep structures', following rules and schemas.

Broadbent's theory implied a spectrum of design approaches, transitioning from the primitive to the industrial: pragmatic to iconic to analogical to canonic. In keeping with the tenets of the Design Methods Movement (Jones 1970) with which his early work is associated, Broadbent was writing about the *processes* of design, but this led to a classification of buildings so derived.

It is easy enough to see the limits of Broadbent's characterisation of both the design process and of the architecture so produced, especially in light of contemporary architectural theory, not least that influenced by Hermeneutics and Deconstruction. Broadbent later took a more critical posture towards his own systematisation with his explorations into Deconstruction (Broadbent and Glusberg 1991).

How did Broadbent reconcile his schema of iconic, pragmatic, analogic and canonic design with Peirce's schema of icon, index and symbol? According to Broadbent, Peirce's sign classes lie on a spectrum, from likeness between the iconic sign and its referent (object) at one end, to the arbitrary association of the symbol at the other. The indexical sign is between these two. Broadbent also positioned the icon and the symbol at extreme ends of a spectrum of lesser to greater perceptual sophistication. An icon accords with direct physiological response; the symbol is a 'culturally sanctioned response' (Broadbent 1980: 319). As I will show in Chapter 3, a close reading of Peirce's classifications concurs with this spectrum. An iconic sign relates to immediate perception. The symbolic is further removed and operates in the realms of spoken and written language, and logic.

Broadbent also wanted to relabel his iconic design approach as 'typologic design', to avoid confusion with Peirce's *iconic* sign classification.

> It seems therefore that my analogic and canonic design types represent different aspects of iconicity whilst my iconic design has little or nothing to do with Peirce's original concept. That is why I now call it Typologic, thus bringing it into that long tradition of design by typology.
>
> (Broadbent 1980: 326)

Broadbent traced iconic (i.e. typologic) design to the architectural traditions of Abé Laugier and Quatremére de Quincy, who championed the idea of building types, and historical lineages showing how one type derived from another, even going as far back as a notion of a 'primitive hut'. Here architecture has something in common with Peirce's use of classification, in particular his classification of signs. The project of identifying building types and their relationships parallels Peirce's project to classify signs. Hence, Peirce offers some appeal to architectural systematisers.

Broadbent, and the anglophone tradition of architectural semiotics seemed to stop short of further analysis of Peirce's sign classification. As I have indicated, Peirce did not stop at three sign classes, and his semiotic schema is even more intricate than the simple idea of the icon, index and symbol. Peirce's sign classifications and their application to architecture require further probing. That is the subject of the next chapter.

One of the advantages of Peirce's approach to signs is that it addresses not only the idea that a work of architecture might operate as a sign system, but the broader issue of how architecture fits within communicative structures of all kinds: communication within design, construction and evaluation processes; buildings, their parts and attributes as communicators, people communicating about buildings, representations of buildings, for example, drawings, models, photographs, sound works. Peirce also provides a framework for thinking about legislation, archives, heritage, ruins, demolition, decay, traces and the myriad sounds of the environment. Peirce also exposes the many different aspects of a sign, and how such components address different aspects of the thing the sign refers to, the object.

Saussure opened architecture to conflict, the struggle of political discourse within and about architecture, without drawing attention to its material presence as something 'real'. Peirce on the other hand, as a realist and a pragmatist, opens the linguistic metaphor in architecture to the materiality and reality of the sign situation. Even if we do not accept Peirce's ideas in total, they lead us to think about architecture and its context in new ways that are both insightful and practical.

CHAPTER 3

Sign-Vehicles

Before delving deeper into Peirce's sign classification, we need to consider some of his terminology, and how it differs from Saussure's. Saussure theorised about the *signifier* and the *signified*. You can think of the signifier as the word (e.g. 'tree'), and the signified as the thing being referred to. The signified may be the tree in my neighbour's garden that I see through the kitchen window, or it could be a generalised tree, or the idea of a tree. But Peirce is more specific than Saussure, and his system more grounded in the idea of a reality outside of language. Whereas Saussure considered two elements in the sign situation, Peirce defined three: (i) the sign-vehicle, (ii) the object and (iii) the interpretant.

In the previous chapter I referred to the weathervane as a sign-vehicle. From my office window in Edinburgh, as I write, I see the weathervane on top of St Giles' Kirk. It consists of pressed sheets of metal cut in the profile of a rooster to form a thin vane and is mounted on a vertical axle that is free to rotate. The simple mechanism ensures that the vane is positioned parallel to the direction of the wind, with the smaller head part of the rooster facing into the wind. The larger and heavier part of the profile brings the vane into line with the angle of least resistance against the wind. I can tell the direction of the wind by observing the weathervane. It functions as a sign of the wind direction.

The *sign-vehicle* is that aspect of the sign that carries its communicative function. In the weathervane example, the sign-vehicle is the pivoting vane, not the profile of the rooster, or the way the device is mounted on the roof, or its material composition (important though they may be for its functioning). What did Peirce mean by the *object*? The object is the thing being referred to, or at least those aspects of the entity being referred to that interest me as observer of the weathervane. For example, a weathervane tells us the direction of the wind, but not the temperature of the air. Wind direction is here the object of the sign.

The *sign-vehicle* is that aspect of the sign that carries its communicative function. The object is the thing being referred to

The *interpretant* is whatever arises from the sign situation. Peirce said, 'the idea in the mind that the sign excites, which is a mental sign of the same object, is called an interpretant of the sign' (Peirce 1998f: 13). In general, any sign situation provokes a result, an interpretation, a translation, an effect or use. We might say this is the meaning of the sign. As a philosophical Pragmatist, Peirce was inclined to think of meaning as in use: 'A word has meaning for us in so far as we are able to make use of it' (Peirce 1998m: 256). Much later, the philosopher Ludwig Wittgenstein (1889–1951) echoed Peirce: 'the meaning of a word is its use in the language' (Wittgenstein 1953: I sec. 43). In the case of the weathervane the *interpretant* captures how we translate the observation into a decision about whether to close the windows, put on a coat, or tell someone the wind is coming from the west. In fact, the interpretant may set off another chain of sign events. The word 'interpretant' seems unique to Peirce's semiotic system. As we shall see, the vehicle-object-interpretant combination is one of many triads in Peirce's semiotic schema.

The *interpretant* is whatever arises from the sign situation.

As we saw in the previous chapter, icons, indices and symbols are classes of signs in Peirce's system. From this simple triadic formulation, he graduated to ten classes of signs. I will follow Peirce's convention and number these with Roman numerals [i–x] in what follows, to make it easier to cross reference them later. I do not think it is essential that the architectural reader absorbs fully, and commits to memory, Peirce's sign classifications. But a bigger picture emerges that is highly relevant to architecture.

Icon

As a development on Peirce's sign classification, consider his expansion on the idea of the icon. His schema defined three subclasses of iconic sign. There are signs that pertain simply to qualities. I mentioned the colour of the weathervane as irrelevant to its function as a sign of the wind direction. In some sign situations the reverse is the case. The quality, that is, the colour of the sign, is more important than other incidental aspects of the sign. A paint colour swatch provides an obvious example of a sign that relates to quality. The swatch indicates what you will find if you buy a particular tin of paint. As the Peircean scholar Albert Atkin points out, it is not the shape of the swatch, or the kind of paper it is printed on that carries the sign function of the swatch, but the colour, as a quality (Atkin 2016: 143). Such a quality is the aspect of a sign that delivers the information irrespective of the medium it appears in. Peirce called this aspect of a sign a *qualisign*. Such a quality can relate to colour, texture, temperature, weight, but also qualities such as beautiful, melancholic, disgusting, and any qualification we may add to that quality – such as not just heavy, but *too* heavy, *too* red, or not red enough. The idea of the *qualisign* is a helpful distinction in the case of architecture. You might say that the Eiffel Tower as a sign-vehicle references other communication towers as its sign objects, other similarly shaped towers for example, but also strength, power, sophistication, nation, or Paris. But then you are entitled to ask, which aspect of the Eiffel Tower operates as the sign-vehicle that delivers the sign function: is it the Eiffel Tower's height, shape, scale, materials, colour, or setting, and in what combination?

As an icon is a resemblance, for this class of sign (an [i] *iconic qualisign*) you are entitled to ask which quality of the sign-vehicle *resembles* which quality of its object? In the case of a drawing (icon) of the Taj Mahal, which qualities of the drawing resemble which aspects of the building as encountered on its site in Uttar Pradesh? Is it the profile, the colour, the light, the mood or other quality? As we shall see in the next section, Peirce's notion of quality is pertinent to a range of sign situations.

Peirce also indicates that iconic signs can be specific or general. In the case of the drawing of the Taj Mahal, the drawing (iconic sign) resembles a specific object as a one-off. A floor plan drawn by a project architect is of a particular building. A map of Edinburgh functions as a sign of that particular place. As such representations are singular, Peirce calls these [ii] *iconic sinsigns* – an abbreviation of iconic 'singular signs'.

There are also signs that are pictorial resemblances of a class of things, such as generalised diagrams that do not belong to any particular instance, for example, a generic typological floor plan diagram of the kind found in Jean-Nicolas-Louis Durand's (1760–1834) neoclassical catalogues of floor plans (Durand 2000). The drawings do not belong to any building in particular, but a class of buildings defined by function, such as hospital, school, library or office building. Such a diagram may also relate to form, such as courtyard, linear, cruciform, circular plan, or tower block. This idea of a diagram as sign refers to a class of things, by virtue of convention. Here it is as if the resemblance is legislated by a rule. Peirce called this case of resemblance, an [v] *iconic legisign*. 'Legisign' is an abbreviation of 'legislated sign'. The 'legislation' may be informal, of course, and such an iconic sign is closer to the idea of a visual schema, a template or a pattern. This idea of the *iconic legisign* matches Broadbent's later amendment of his *iconic* classification to the 'Typologic sign': a generalised diagram as the basis of a design, that follows a grid, building system, convention or template.

To summarise these subclassifications of the iconic sign, there are icons that are *qualisigns*, *sinsigns* and *legisigns*. An iconic sign works with resemblance. But that

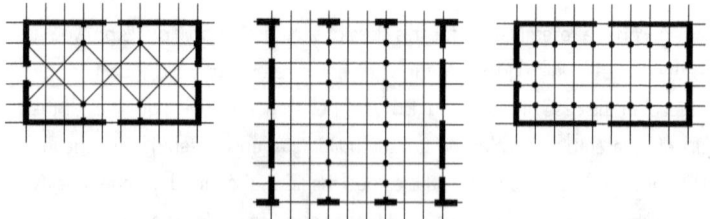

Figure 6 Typological portico plan diagrams, after Durand (2000).
Source: Author.

resemblance presents qualities that in turn refer to the qualities of its object, or the iconic sign can refer to an individual object, or it can refer to a class or set of objects. As with all his classifications we may ask if these classes are discrete. Do they overlap, and do they cover all interesting cases of the icon? Why just three and not four or five subclassifications? I will explain Peirce's overall triadic schema later, and the importance of the number three. All three descriptors (*qualisign*, *sinsign* and *legisign*) also pertain to the index and the symbol, as we shall explore next.

Index

So far, I have discussed icons. A weathervane with its vane in the shape of a rooster serves as an iconic sign of a rooster due to the resemblance it bears to that object, at least in terms of certain qualities such as profile, silhouette, positioning and scale. What about the weathervane's role as an indexical sign? If it is functioning properly, a weathervane points in the direction of the wind by virtue of its orientation to the wind, aided by the profile of the vane and its pivoting axis. An indexical sign relates to its object, in this case the wind direction, not by resemblance, but by *deriving* from its object.

Consider the relationship between smoke and fire, another of Peirce's examples. Smoke acts as a sign of a fire. It is possible to establish (iconic) resemblances between any two objects, but we are unlikely to think of smoke, or any of its qualities, *resembling* the fire from which it emanates. Smoke is not usually hot, yellow, flickering, or consuming, like fire. Smoke is an indicator of fire, that is, an index, as most observant adults recognise a causal connection between fire and smoke. A crack in a wall is an indexical sign of settlement in the foundations and does not necessarily resemble that underlying condition. A weathervane functions as a sign of the wind direction by virtue of the inevitable connection between its mechanism and the wind. The angle of the vane does not *resemble* the wind, as if an icon. Think also of an explosion, as in the violent and incendiary destruction of a building. The after-effects of an explosion do not necessarily resemble the explosion. So, the effects of an explosion would be in the indexical sign class. Dust and ruins are indexical signs of an explosion and derive inevitably from it. Note that Peirce was keen not to tie the indexical sign to its object as always causal, as if an object *causes* its indexical sign. He established three subclassifications of the indexical sign that help explain this decoupling.

I have already mentioned the iconic *legisign* as a characteristic of an iconic sign. A *legisign* follows a convention or rule. A helpful online article by cultural theorist Nicole Everaert-Desmedt provides some examples of *indexical legisigns*: 'passwords, insignias, tickets for a show, traffic signals, and the words of a language' (Everaert-Desmedt 2011). *Legisigns* are a general class of signs pertaining to language, that is, spoken and written words, but not limited to such cases. As discussed in the previous section, icons can also be *legisigns*, but here I am just considering *indexical legisigns*. Peirce adopted a further uncommon term for aspects of a sign that are incomplete. These are *rhemes*. A *rheme* (i.e. a rhematic sign) is a part of a statement in language, a part of a proposition that needs the full proposition to make sense. I think that the *rheme* is the most difficult of Peirce's terms, and I will explain its various meanings further on in this chapter. For the moment it is sufficient to think of a *rheme* as a sign that is incomplete without knowing its context. For Peirce, pronouns are *rhemes*: such as 'he', 'she', 'it', 'him', 'her', 'this', 'that' and 'those'. These words are indexical *legisigns* as they rely on conventions or rules to function as signs, in this case the grammar of the language provides such rules. Pronouns are also *rhemes*: [vi] *rhematic indexical legisigns*, in that they are incomplete. After all, unconnected pronouns lead to ambiguity: for example, 'He said he would go to his house'. The pronoun 'he' in this case could refer to one person or three different people, or just two people. Signs that are *rhemes* require further signs to settle ambiguity and to deliver their interpretant function, in other words to be meaningful. I am here discussing indexicals, but according to Peirce, all *iconic* signs are *rhemes*. I will explain how in a later part of this chapter.

A page number locator in the index at the end of this book is a [vi] *rhematic indexical legisign*. A page number is a *rheme* in that it needs accompanying words, phrases and headings in order to function, that is, to deliver its interpretant. The page number locator is an indexical sign in that it relates to its object (the relevant page of the book) via a procedure, process or algorithm, and not through resemblance. There is a process in play whereby you flick through the pages of the book to find the relevant page and its content, a practice or convention that has to be learned or programmed. In digital formats the link to the relevant page is usually automated through hyperlinks. An item in a book index is a *legisign* as you need to know the conventions of the numbering system in use and the language of the system. The indexical sign is a key element of any use an architect might make of an archive, not to mention schedules, spreadsheets and databases, and their search and lookup algorithms.

Already, I suspect some readers will be overwhelmed by these fine distinctions. I will summarise the implications towards the end of this chapter. In the meantime, simply note the intricacy of Peirce's system of signs. I also include a list of these terms in the glossary.

Peirce provided further qualifications to the indexical sign class. Whereas a *rheme* is incomplete without other signs, a *dicent* is complete and self-contained. That is an indexical sign that is a simple statement delivering complete information about the object it refers to. So, a cry or call out from someone selling goods at a market or from a street vendor is this kind of *dicent indexical* sign. Specifically, it is [vii] a *dicent indexical legisign*, as when someone calls out the name of the magazine they are selling: for example, 'Big Issue!' The sign is complete (*dicent*) in that it delivers its sign function without further qualification. A *rheme* is incomplete, but a *dicent* is a complete statement tying a *rheme* to its object. The call of the street vendor is an *index* in that it references its object other than through resemblance, and it is a *legisign* in that you need to know the language being spoken and the verbal conventions of the street crier. Peirce used this example of the call of the street vendor, which serves as a rudimentary example of the everyday use of words and language.

If these distinctions seem obscure in the case of architecture, think of the way sound functions to define space. In a study, with colleagues, into sound in physical environments, we explored how such primitive vocalisations in public space serve to define territory, to assert a claim on space. In this light the cry of the street seller indexes a space. We also maintained that it is not just the cry that affirms the space, but its repetition, and patterns in that repetition, as different actors compete for attention, and assert their claims (Coyne 2010: 93–6). In that study, we did not identify them as such, but the uses of the voice to claim space are examples of [vii] *dicent indexical legisigns*.

An indexical sign might also include a raw, spontaneous cry that does not belong to any particular language convention, such as the cry of a baby, a shriek of pain or a laugh. These are specific vocalisations that are outside of convention, that is, their use and interpretation does not draw substantially on learning. Peirce was mainly concerned with spoken language and other audible signs, but we could extend such communications to gestures and other bodily movements. These spontaneous vocalisations and gestures are [iv] *dicent indexical sinsigns*. Peirce was thinking here of something visceral and embodied. I think of a person's response on encountering a spectacular space or view: a cry of amazement, or an intake of breath, an open mouth, raised arms, or a lifting of the head, a response often exercised in an encounter with sublime spaces, for example on entering a cathedral or beholding a view from a mountain top. Other environments and moods elicit different examples of [iv] *dicent indexical sinsigns*: the sighs that accompany gloomy and melancholic events and places, the groans uttered by those frustrated designers and building users under stress, and the laughter of children at play.

Symbol

Peirce's third basic sign classification is that of the symbol. The idea of the symbolic sign addresses how we commonly think of utterances in language. In the symbolic sign classification, we have common nouns (house, car, tree) as they appear in sentences, not as singular terms shouted by a street vendor. A symbolic sign is a *rheme* if it is part of an utterance, and if it requires the context of its sentence or phrase to deliver its interpretant function. In full, this class defines a [viii] *rhematic symbolic legisign*. Nouns fit this classification. Columns, windows and doors in a building are similar to nouns in a sentence, and are related by syntactic rules, that is, grammars. Any word category (noun, verb, pronoun, article or key word) is subject to syntactic rules. We could say that building components relate readily to nouns as they are commonly identified by nouns. I mentioned book indexes in the previous section. Surely, they involve symbols. A book index commonly includes both [vi] *rhematic indexical legisigns* and [viii] *rhematic symbolic legisigns*, that is, both page number locators and nouns (or key words).

Symbolic signs can also be truth statements. Assertions that someone could potentially claim to be true or at least can be tested are [ix] *dicent symbolic legisigns*. Such statements include 'the sky is blue', 'it sometimes snows in December', 'lithium atoms have 3 electrons'. Such statements are straightforward assertions in logic. A table of facts about a building would fall under this category, as in a schedule or database, but any assertion in language is a [ix] *dicent symbolic legisign*.

There are also signs that we would normally think of as collections of symbols, or generalised statements. These signs tell people what to do, and the consequences if they don't follow the instructions. These are rules of inference: 'if there are no clouds then the sky will be blue'; 'all dogs are mammals'; 'when the swallows fly high the weather will be dry'; 'all habitable rooms must have a window'. Peirce called these signs *arguments*. By 'argument' Peirce meant statements that get passed between interlocutors in a spirited conversation, as when someone says, 'what is your argument'? In mathematics and logic, an argument is also a symbol in a formula or logical predicate. To avoid this confusion (or add to it) Peirce also described this sign classification as a *delome*, a term that is not in the OED. I will stay with 'argument' here. To complete the set of triads, Peirce called this class of sign an [x] *argument symbolic legisign*, though he simplifies that to [x] *argument* as I will explain in the next section.

Ten classes of signs

At this stage in the discussion it is worth noting the breadth and complexity of Peirce's sign classification system. A second point is that any sign situation exhibits several characteristics. The idea of the *sign-vehicle* captures that. So far in this chapter I have attempted to explain Peirce's system from the point of view of the three primary classifications of icon, index and symbol. Table 3.1 provides a summary of Peirce's classifications, with examples.

The way Peirce derived these ten classes requires further explanation. Recall his definitions of *interpretant*, *object* and *sign-vehicle*. Here is his explanation of the *object* and *interpretant*.

> **I define a sign as anything which is so determined by something else, called its Object, and so determines an effect upon a person, which effect I call its interpretant, that the latter is thereby mediately determined by the former.**
> **(Peirce 1998g: 478)**

As we have seen, Peirce thought of a sign as somehow emerging from its object. Put another way, the sign is 'determined' by its object. This is already a naturalistic way of looking at signs. Signs come at us from the world around us. For Peirce the pragmatist, the result when a sign does its work is to produce an effect on the agent (a human being or other organism) who identifies the sign. For Peirce, the major component of the sign situation is the practical effect, hence his use of the term *interpretant*. The *sign-vehicle* is that component of the object that delivers the sign. Note that Peirce did not use the term 'sign-vehicle' but others have, and the term avoids some ambiguity in Peirce's terminology (Atkin 2016: 129). He distributes his nine sign descriptors across interpretant, object and sign-vehicle. Table 3.2 shows the interpretant, object and sign-vehicle as rows, along with their descriptors (*rheme*, *dicent*, etc.).

<u>**the major component of the sign situation is the practical effect, hence his use of the term *interpretant*.**</u>

Returning to Table 3.1, note that there are ten classes (or subclasses) of signs, labelled in Roman numerals [i] to [x]. To be useful, these descriptors should account for every kind of sign you might encounter, and they should be general across all disciplines and communication systems. Even if they are so inclusive, we might question their usefulness as sign classifications in architecture. As suggested by Broadbent's discussion (Chapter 2), iconic signs are of great relevance in particular diagrams, drawings and plans, and these have received most attention in architectural discourse. But in his *Handbook of Semiotics*, Nöth referenced the German scholar Elisabeth Walther (Walther 1974) who identified architectural signs primarily in terms of *indexes*.

> **Walther determines the factually existing building as a dicent indexical sinsign. Being a singular object fixed with respect to time and space makes it a sinsign. By referring to the architect who designed it, the building becomes an index, and as a cultural object which evokes judgements and evaluations, the building is a dicent.**
>
> **(Nöth 1990: 438)**

I will develop the importance of the index in the next chapter. Can any of these classes and subclasses be merged, and could Peirce have created further classes or subclasses within these? His classification of signs is intriguing not least due to the process by which he derived these ten classes, which was not due entirely to an observation of how signs work, but his system of threes.

You will see in Table 3.1 that I have included Peirce's terms for each of the ten sign classes. These correspond to the terms in Table 3.2, providing three terms for each of the three rows. Rather than ten classes, we would expect all possible combinations of 3 by 3 indicated in Table 3.2 to yield 27 possible combinations. According to Peirce's system the 17 combinations that he leaves out are impossible, or at least by implication, meaningless. In order to explain this, I need to reintroduce yet another triad that I mentioned only in passing in Chapter 1. The sign classes derive from Peirce's view that being-in-the-world has three aspects, simply labelled Firstness, Secondness and Thirdness. I will follow Peirce's convention of capitalising these terms.

Table 3.1 Summary of Peirce's main classification of signs.

	Definition	Example	Peirce's terms for this class of sign
Icon	A sign-vehicle as a quality	Something is red, though we have not yet settled on the object to which this applies	[i] Rhematic Iconic **Qualisign**
	A diagram, drawing or painting of a specific object	A drawing of my house; a map of Edinburgh	[ii] Rhematic **Iconic Sinsign**
	A generalised diagram of a class of objects	A grid for organising a building layout; Durand's diagram of a generalised portico building type	[v] Rhematic **Iconic Legisign**
Index	A raw spontaneous cry or gesture outside of a language convention	An audible sigh on encountering a melancholic space or circumstance; exclamations and gestures on entering a cathedral or other sublime space	[iii] **Rhematic Indexical Sinsign**
	A sign that emerges from its object	Smoke (from a fire); a weathervane turned to the wind; a photograph	[iv] **Dicent** Indexical **Sinsign**
	A demonstrative pronoun	He, she, it	[vi] **Rhematic Indexical Legisign**
	A cry that draws attention by convention, e.g. street seller's cry	Big Issue! Warning! Help!	[vii] **Dicent Indexical Legisign**

Table 3.1 (Cont.)

	Definition	Example	Peirce's terms for this class of sign
Symbol	A common noun	House, door, window	[viii] **Rhematic Symbol** Legisign
	A proposition that can be claimed as true or false	The house is new; the flat is 120 square metres	[ix] **Dicent Symbol** Legisign
	A rule of inference	All habitable rooms need an opening for ventilation	[x] **Argument** Symbolic Legisign

Note: The terms in bold are those that Peirce thought sufficient to distinguish the sign classes from each other.

First, Second, Third

Firstness is the raw quality of a thing: 'The first is that whose being is simply in itself, not referring to anything nor lying behind anything' (Peirce 1992e: 248). He elaborated:

> **What the world was to Adam on the day he opened his eyes to it, before he had drawn any distinctions, or had become conscious of his own existence,—that is first, present, immediate, fresh, new, initiative, original, spontaneous, free, vivid, conscious, and evanescent.**
>
> (1992e: 248)

Table 3.2 Components of the sign situation and how they relate to Peirce's nine sign descriptors

Interpretant	**Rheme**	**Dicent**	**Argument (Delome)**	
The effect on someone who comprehends or interprets the sign	A part of a meaningful expression	A complete expression	A proposition that serves as a rule or generalisation	The rheme, dicent and argument have a direct bearing on the meaning of the sign
Object	**Icon**	**Index**	**Symbol**	
The thing that is being referred to; i.e. that generates the sign	A resemblance	A sign emanating from its object, sometimes causally connected	An expression that is general and abstract	The icon, index and symbol focus on the importance of the object within the sign situation
Sign-vehicle	**Qualisign**	**Sinsign**	**Legisign**	
That component of the sign that refers to the object	A quality of something independent of the thing it refers to	A singular, specific instance of a sign	A conventional expression for which someone needs to know the language	Qualisign, sinsign and legisign relate to particular properties of the sign

Firstness includes our immediate response to the quality of a thing. Peirce uses the example of 'a feeling of "red"' (1992e: 248). I would include what Heidegger said (with no reference to Peirce) of a person's active engagement with objects in the world, as when a carpenter driving a nail into a piece of wood feels that the hammer they are wielding is too heavy or too light. I would add the immediate feeling we have when outdoors of the wind as cold, bracing, too warm, dry or gusty. Such qualitative experiences do not need to be expressed in words or gestures in order to have their effect as signs. Peirce identified the *rheme*, the icon and the *qualisign* (i.e. an incomplete sign, a resemblance and a quality) in terms of Firstness.

If you think of a *rheme* as a spontaneous and unattributed qualitative experience, then it fits Peirce's characterisation of Firstness. Probing the idea of the *rheme* further, Peirce conflated notions of incompleteness and quality in the *rheme*. Linguists and literary scholars discuss the *rheme* as it relates to the *theme* of a sentence. The theme of a sentence is the part that you already understand, by virtue of what has gone before or as the subject of the sentence. A *rheme* is something supplemental to that, some additional information, or a comment. 'I wandered' is a theme; 'lonely as a cloud that floats on high o'er vales and hills' is a *rheme* (in the first line of a poem by William Wordsworth). If you do not know the theme of the sentence (wandering), then it is unlikely that the *rheme* (supplementary comment) will make sense. The *rheme* needs the theme. As in many cases, the *rheme* in this line of poetry is experiential and qualitative. Peirce and his commentators provided examples of *rhemes* such as '__ is red', '__ is a blue-eyed cat', '__ is happy', where the underscore indicates the as-yet unspecified theme of the sentence (Atkin 2016: 145).

I think that architectural theorists would replace the theme-*rheme* structure by the more applicable concept of *metaphor*. So, Le Corbusier's famous metaphorical statement, 'A house is a machine for living', presents 'house' as the theme, with 'is a machine for living' as the *rheme*. In this case the second term of the house-machine metaphor, the *rheme*, is incomplete without the theme. Peirce does not elaborate on metaphor in terms of the *rheme* but does think of metaphor as an example of an icon (Anderson 1984).

According to Peirce, all *iconic* signs belong to Firstness. Anyone open to the immediacy of visual experience will recognise when one thing resembles another, as when a drawing of a house (as iconic sign) resembles the house next door (as object). Recognition, resemblance and metaphor fall well within the purview of Firstness – an immediate childlike delight at similitude and coincidence. All iconic signs are also *rhemes* according to Peirce. That fits his general description of Firstness and the *rheme*. The resemblance between an icon and its object is based on identified *qualities*.

The isolation and recognition of a quality (*qualisign*) independently of the object exhibiting the quality is similarly grounded in the immediacy of Firstness. I think this connection is easiest to grasp in Peirce's schema, as his definitions of Firstness focus on such immediate experiential qualities.

In spite of the linguistic subtlety of the definitions above, Firstness is primarily about raw experience that defies ready expression. In fact, Peirce finishes the definition of Firstness by stating, 'Only, remember that every description of it must be false to it' (Peirce 1992e: 248). On the other hand, Peirce's categories of Secondness and Thirdness clearly pertain to signs as commonly understood and identified, that is, overt expressions in language, gestures and symbols. Secondness includes facts derived from Firstness, or assertions about an imagined Firstness: a cry, a declaration, a sentence, a premise in a logical argument. It was important to Peirce that such statements do not exist in isolation, but depend on Firstness: 'the Second is precisely that which cannot be without the first. It meets us in such facts as Another, Relation, Compulsion, Effect, Dependence, Independence, Negation, Occurrence, Reality, Result' (1992e: 248).

Peirce provided three cases of Secondness: the *dicent*, the index and the *sinsign*. As discussed already, the *dicent* is that characteristic of a sign that is complete and self-contained. An indexical sign derives directly from its object. A *sinsign* is that aspect of a sign that operates as a singular sign, a one-off, as opposed to a sign that refers to a class of objects. Signs that draw on Secondness are not the raw thing (Firstness), but a representation of it, or a pointer to it.

Thirdness includes those complex propositions or sets of propositions derived from Firstness and Secondness. Thirdness is exemplified by a simple rule that relates an entity in Firstness with an entity in Secondness: 'that which bridges over the chasm between the absolute first and last, and that brings them into relationship' (Peirce 1992e: 249). Thirdness includes statements in language, whether spoken or written, or a more idiosyncratic language of symbols or other conventions. Peirce included abstract symbols, pronouns, street cries, ordinary nouns, propositions and discursive arguments in general. Thirdness therefore includes signs as commonly understood as linguistic elements, and includes within this category signs that are arguments, symbols and *legisigns*. Arguments are discussion points. Symbols are words, their proxies, or elements in a mathematical equation, and *legisigns* are signs that depend on conventions, rules, grammars and other learned practices. Any sign situation may have elements of Firstness, Secondness or Thirdness.

Table 3.3 shows the 3×3 graph of Table 3.2 as a grid with columns labelled for Firstness, Secondness and Thirdness (1st, 2nd and 3rd). The rows are labelled according to the three elements of the sign: sign-vehicle, object and interpretant. I have labelled the rows in that order from the bottom row to the top. Peirce thought of the object as derived from the sign-vehicle, and the interpretant as derived from both the sign-vehicle and the object.

The table shows a 3×3 grid. Considering one from each row, there are 27 possible combinations of interpretant, object and sign-vehicle, which makes 27 sign classes.

Table 3.3 Simplification of Table 3.2. Selecting one item from each row in turn results in 27 combinations

Interpretant	Rheme	Dicent	Argument (Delome)
Object	Icon	Index	Symbol
Sign-vehicle	Qualisign	Sinsign	Legisign
	1st	2nd	3rd

If you look back at Peirce's ten sign categories summarised in Table 3.1, you will see that they are derived from the combinations made possible in Table 3.3, such as [i] *rhematic iconic qualisign*, [ii] *rhematic iconic sinsign*, [v] *rhematic iconic legisign*, [iii] *rhematic indexical sinsign*, [iv] *dicent indexical sinsign*, etc.

It is important that Peirce did not admit every combination into his system. For example, a *dicent iconic legisign* is excluded. A compelling explanation of how Peirce derived ten from 27 possible combinations seems to have eluded many of Peirce's commentators. After a paragraph explaining Peirce's system, Atkins concluded succinctly: 'This leaves us with ten permissible combinations among sign-vehicle, object and interpretant, and, so, ten possible kinds of signs' (Atkin 2016: 147). He followed this with a table similar to my Table 3.1 above. Atkin then raised a question about the system's usefulness: 'How useful such a typology might prove to be is an open question, and even Peirce shows a tendency to treat it as a matter of simply tracing out the full implications of his account of signs' (Atkin 2016: 148). Indeed, the derivation of ten from 27 appears arbitrary, unless you are prepared to buy into Peirce's categories of Firstness, Secondness and Thirdness. I will attempt to explain the derivation of Peirce's ten classes of signs in what follows.

It turns out that the categories of Firstness, Secondness and Thirdness are crucial in defining what makes a sign, in particular the dependencies between these categories. Peirce excluded 17 of these combinations due to the dependencies between Firstness, Secondness and Thirdness. Thirdness can depend on Second and Firstness, and Secondness can depend on Firstness. But Firstness cannot depend on Secondness or Thirdness and Secondness cannot depend on Thirdness. This difficult schema comes down to a simple configurational rule. The rule says that a path joining cells in Table 3.3 from bottom to top must exclude paths that stray into the right of the column they start in. I explained further the derivation of the ten sign classes in some detail in a blog post (Coyne 2017), and present a suggestive diagram of this process here. The 3×3 configurations of circles correspond to the grid cells in Table 3.3, and the lines connecting them show the combinations allowed by Peirce's schema. I have greyed out the combinations that do not conform.

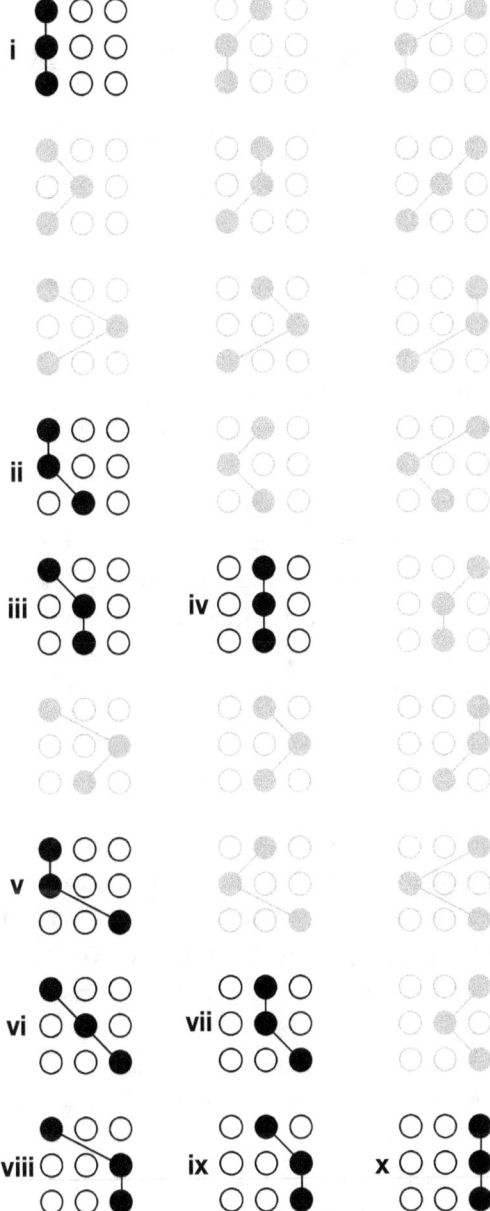

Figure 7 Derivation of Peirce's sign classifications: 27 combinations of 3x3 descriptors reduced to ten on the basis of his theory of dependencies between Firstness, Secondness and Thirdness.
Source: Author.

the categories of Firstness, Secondness and Thirdness are crucial in defining what makes a sign, in particular the dependencies between these categories.

Breaking the rules

Peirce's schema raises questions. The ten classes of signs exclude 17 other combinations. Such exclusivity is bound to fascinate anyone interested in breaking boundaries and who is untethered to the sanctity of Peirce's scheme. Consider the excluded *dicent iconic legisign* classification. Such a sign might be a statement about something that also resembles its object according to some rule or convention. Perhaps that is where words get arranged on a page to look like the thing they represent: word pictures, or certain forms of street graffiti. As far as I am aware, Peirce did not consider such sign cases and visual puns, though he did exhibit a propensity for textual and visual jokes in his articles and private notes (Leja 2000).

Another case Peirce did not seem to entertain is how raw feelings get influenced and moderated by spoken language, that is, how Thirdness might precede Firstness. That would be something like a *delomic indexical qualisign*. Peirce did not seem to include that possibility in his schema. I think that would be a qualitative impression (e.g. of anger) (Firstness) where we think of that construction as already formed in language (Thirdness). Some contemporary theorists of the emotions have argued that the definition of an emotion, and even the raw feeling of it, can derive from an argument in language (de Rivera and Grinkis 1986). Think of how the press media might identify anger amongst the voters, or the euphoria of the crowd. Not only might we feel something because reports tell us that is how we feel, but to use the emotion in such reports serves a political purpose, and it identifies a feeling that no individual may actually feel. In the experience of architecture think of how feelings about a space are frequently primed by expectations derived from what we have

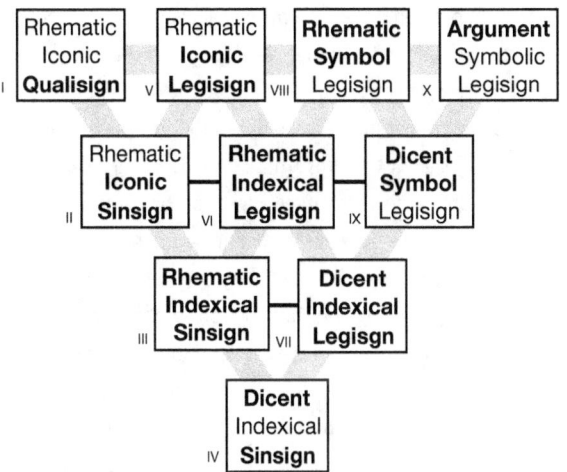

Figure 8 Peirce's sign classifications and their interdependencies (Peirce 1998e: 296).
Source: Author.

read or heard about the space. Prior presentations in the media, online and in books of the nearly completed Sagrada Familia in Barcelona are complicit in the delight, awe, or even disappointment we feel on entering the building for the first time.

It seems as though Peirce's schema limits, in certain respects, what might be considered a sign. Another way of looking at any shortcomings in Peirce's system is to say that it brings certain characteristics of the sign and being into sharp relief by virtue of what it excludes as well as includes.

<u>Another way of looking at any shortcomings in Peirce's system is to say that it brings certain characteristics of the sign and being into sharp relief by virtue of what it excludes as well as includes.</u>

The apogee of Peirce's complicated system is a pyramidal diagram. This diagram has interesting properties. You do not even need to know what the terms in the boxes mean to grasp the symmetry of this geometry. The numbered squares are displayed in the figure such that those joined by a thick grey line are alike in two respects, that is, they share two terms. Those squares joined by a thin black line are alike in only one respect. The three apexes of the triangle (top left, top right and the bottom) have no terms in common with the squares on the opposite side of the triangle. They are diametrically opposed categories. In his original version of the diagram, from which this is copied, there are terms in the squares that are in a lighter font. I have reproduced that distinction in Figure 8 and Table 1. Peirce said these lighter terms are superfluous and can be discarded as you don't need them to discriminate between the squares. So, it is sufficient to label the bottom square a *dicent sinsign*, as there is no other square with those two terms. On the other hand, the central square needs to retain its three terms: [vi] *rhematic indexical legisign*, as there are other sign categories around it that share two of its terms. The central sign category [vi] acts as a kind of pivot. In fact, a *rhematic indexical legisign* is an indexical sign as generally understood independently of Peirce's schema. The word 'that', known as an indexical or a demonstrative pronoun in grammar, provides a good example, as does any other means of deliberately pointing something out – with a finger for example. The 'legisign' term in the category description reminds us that there is some convention to the method of pointing. Like terms in language, it has to be learned. There is nothing in the word 'that' hinting at what we are referring to. The other categories seem to orbit around that basic linguistic sign category.

Examples at the apex of the inverted pyramid: [iv] *dicent indexical sinsign*, would include smoke from a fire, a weathervane turned to the wind, or a photograph. According to Peirce,

> a **Dicent Sinsign** is any object of direct experience in so far as it is a sign, and, as such affords information concerning its Object. This it can only do by being really affected by its Object; so that it is necessarily an Index.
>
> (1998e: 294)

A *dicent* is a complete qualitative expression (e.g. the object is bright, sad, loud or melancholic). As an indexical the sign does not resemble its source (object) but appears to be caused by it. As a *sinsign* it is a singular non-linguistic event. Added together, a loud bang from an obvious source would qualify.

Peirce's classification of signs has generated much industry demonstrated not least by countless web sites, some interactive, that seek to explore and explain his system and its implications. For an intriguing expansion of Peirce's diagram see the interactive website: *Minute Semeiotic* (Romanini 2009). The site also explains each of the boxes on Peirce's pyramid. For example, drawing on Peirce, the *Minute Semeiotic* site explains the sign category: [iv] *dicent indexical sinsign*, as being:

> the final shocking effect produced by an unexpected and strident sound communicating that some existent thing nearby is emitting such sound; ... it is the interpreter understanding the assertion 'There is here and now an unexpected and strident sound' and reacting accordingly to the asserted; the final product of mechanical communication among the pieces of a machine (the movement produced by the energy transmission); the final effect produced by the transmission of a pulse (the starting up of a computer, for instance).

<u>Peirce's classification of signs has generated much industry demonstrated not least by countless web sites, some interactive, that seek to explore and explain his system and its implications.</u>

Its positioning on the pyramid puts this class of sign as something raw, immediate, sudden, emanating from the object, with an obvious cause, with immediately accessible qualities, and that does not look or sound like its source: a flash of light from a faulty circuit, an explosion from a firecracker, the sound of a tray of dishes crashing to the floor, a pile driver doing its work on a construction site, the demolition of a building. Such machinations put me in mind of Filippo Tommaso Marinetti's (1876–1944) *Futurist Manifesto* (Marinetti 1909), and Luigi Russolo's (1885–1947) *The Art of Noise*, which celebrated

> the gurglings of water, air and gas inside metallic pipes, the rumblings and rattlings of engines breathing with obvious animal spirits, the rising and falling of pistons, the stridency of mechanical saws, the loud jumping of trolleys on their rails, the snapping of whips, the whipping of flags.
>
> (Russolo 2004: 7)

Returning to Saussure's Structuralism for a moment, the structural understanding of signs outlined in Chapter 2 amplified the agonistics of opposites. Peirce's semiotics admits the materiality of ambient noise, the sounds of construction and destruction.

<u>Peirce's semiotics admits the materiality of ambient noise, the sounds of construction and destruction.</u>

The number three

It is no coincidence that Peirce settled on three as a starting point for his classification of the sign, or numbers derived from three. In Chapter 2, I indicated that one of the major differences between Structuralism and Peirce's semiotics resides in the numbers two and three. Structuralism is a philosophy of twos, binary oppositions by which language phenomena are reduced to relationships between two entities, for example, the signifier and the signified, or opposites. As I have shown, Peirce was a declared philosopher of threes, and he attached much significance to threeness, the triad, in his thinking.

Not all of Peirce's papers had been published by the time of his death. Editors have since collected his papers into an eight-volume compendium (Peirce 1965). But as I mentioned in the Introduction, the only place we see explicit reference to architecture in Volumes 1 and 2 of *The Essential Pierce*, occurs in the essay, 'The Architecture of Theories' (Peirce 1992b), in which he asserted, 'the studies preliminary to the construction of a great theory should be at least as deliberate and thorough as those that are preliminary to the building of a dwelling-house'

(Peirce 1992e: 286). The preliminary theory to which he referred is none other than an understanding of the world based on the three categories or aspects to which I have referred: Firstness, Secondness and Thirdness. Here I wish simply to reinforce the priority he accorded to triads. In his justification for dealing with the concept of the sign via three categories, Peirce wrote:

> **Perhaps I might begin by noticing how different numbers have found their champions. Two was extolled by Pater Ramus, Four by Pythagoras, Five by Sir Thomas Browne, and so on. For my part, I am determined foe of no innocent number; I respect and esteem them all their several ways; but I am forced to confess to a leaning to the number three in philosophy.**
> (Peirce 1992e: 247)

Peirce made no reference to Vitruvius or the architectural canon, but ten and its relationship to three has served as a number of some significance in architecture (Vitruvius 1960). Ten of anything implies that the set is complete and finished. This, at least, is the account given by scholar Indra McEwen of the Pythagorean legacy on which the architectural theorist Marcus Vitruvius Pollio (c. 70–15BC) drew in writing his *Ten Books of Architecture* (McEwen 2003). McEwen argued that the division of Vitruvius's text into ten is contrived, and the content could have been otherwise divided. But the ancient Roman scholar was bound to aim for ten, as the number reflected the perfection of nature. Ten is also convenient. Ten cylindrical objects, like scrolls, stack to make an isosceles triangle, and can

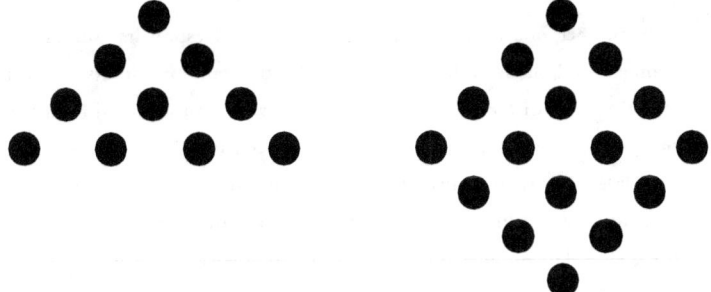

Figure 9 A single and a double tetractys.
Source: Author.

be arranged easily into a perfect equilateral triangle. To the Pythagoreans, this configuration made up the tetractys, the sum of four numbers 1+2+3+4=10 and is 'the source of all things' (according to the OED). The configuration conveniently delivers both threeness (it makes a triangle) and fourness (four items to a side). Instead of stacked scrolls, think of pebbles. If these are spaced in squares then you get a right-angled triangle, which is on the way to forming a double tetractys, a 4×4 square with 16 elements.

Vitruvius also defined architecture's three pillars as firmness, commodity and delight (*firmitas, utilitas, venustas*). As yet I have read of no one aligning these categories with Peirce's Firstness, Secondness and Thirdness, though 'delight' reads as an immediate qualitative feeling about a work of architecture (Firstness). Variously ordered triads so identified frequently show a progression from one end of a spectrum or array to the other. Heidegger's 'Building, Dwelling, Thinking' (Heidegger 1971) and *Poetry, Language, Thought* (Heidegger 1981) each imply a progression from the qualitative, tangible and ordinary to a more profound thought. Peirce's triadic theories also exploit such progressions.

In case we think that Peirce's self-confessed obsession with the number three, and its derivatives, is a naïve nineteenth-century numerological quirk, the contemporary philosopher Graham Harman has provided an interesting outline of the role of number across the spectrum of philosophical thinking, starting with the number one of the monists, who see the universe as an indivisible whole, to the so-called fourfold as promoted by Heidegger.

> The number one is the password of monism. Despite its comforting promise of holistic unity, it tends to be too sanguine in its implicit assertion that difference and strife are less real than a primal harmony of things. The number two seems to announce a conflict of two opposite principles. But such dualism turns out to be paradoxically monotonous, since usually nothing occurs but a constant struggle back and forth across the divide. The number three seems more sophisticated, with its claim to unify two opposed principles in a dynamic third term that both preserves and transcends the crucial features of the two opposite terms.
>
> (Harman 2011: 79)

Harman favours *fourness*, which he thinks maintains the characteristic antagonism of a dualism, but 'avoids the intrinsic monotony of this struggle by spreading it onto a second axis, creating a rich tension between four roles of the world' (2011: 79). Harman makes no reference here to Peirce, but it is apparent that Peirce belongs within the camp of threeness; Structuralism is amongst the twos. Within Harman's identification of numbers lies the suggestion of a geometry. The number four pertains to a cross-axial grid, or a square. In the case of Peirce's threes, the geometrical correlate is a triangle, and as we have seen, that figure recurs throughout Peirce's thinking about the sign.

In the case of most philosophies, the reader could be excused for glossing over any geometrical scaffold by which ideas are delivered. The content is more important than the container; the object supported is more significant than the frame. Scholars with a Structuralist leaning do not necessarily focus their thinking on the particularities of binaries, but on the circumstances of their study, as they pertain to society, politics and psychology. A scholar informed by Peircean semiotics might also focus on what is communicated rather than the supposed triangular relationships Peirce claimed inhere within the sign.

Unlike scholars in communications and media studies, and other design disciplines, the authors in *Signs, Symbols and Architecture*, Broadbent amongst them, did not plumb the depths of Peirce's commitment to threes and its attendant cognitive scaffolding, though other scholars have. As an avowed advocate of the number three as an organising principle for his thoughts, Peirce wrote substantially on the subject of the triad.

As an avowed advocate of the number three as an organising principle for his thoughts, Peirce wrote substantially on the subject of the triad.

It cannot be regarded as incidental to his philosophy.

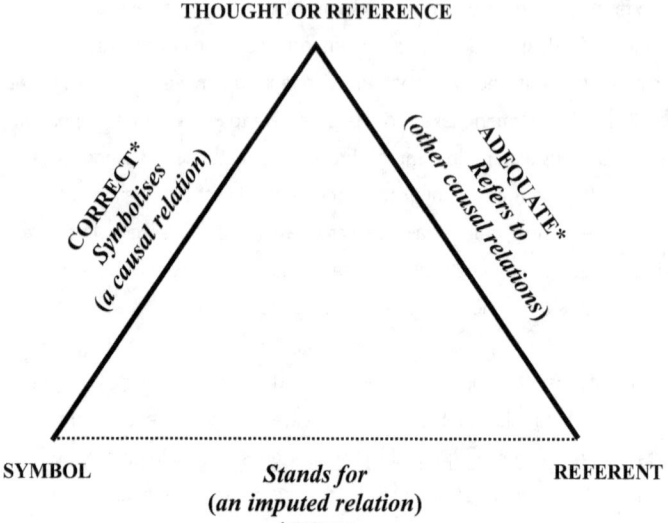

Figure 10 Ogden and Richard's semiotic triangle, after Ogden and Richards (1989).
Source: Author.

I have implied that the main source of semiotic understanding in architecture comes through Structuralism, with Peirce as a late twentieth-century addition. Of course, Peirce came to architecture indirectly through other sources, though not necessarily recognised by those who adopted those sources. One such source is the influential book *The Meaning of Meaning* by C.K. Ogden and I.A. Richards, published in 1923 (Ogden and Richards 1989). They cited both Saussure and Peirce, but they devoted a ten-page appendix to a discussion of Peirce's theories of the sign. Peirce was an obvious influence on their theories, not least in their adoption of a form of the triadic relationship. Though Peirce is scarcely mentioned in *The Meaning of Architecture*, Ogden and Richard's semiotic triangle appears several times, with the apices of the triangle and its sides labelled variously. I have redrawn Ogden and Richard's diagram above (Ogden and Richards 1989: 11).

Architectural readers who might question the relevance of Peirce's classification of signs (beyond icon, index and symbol), can at least wonder at Peirce's formal inventiveness, and learn from that. That formal resourcefulness spurred my initial foray into the topic of Peircean semiotics. It appeals to anyone with an interest in geometry, programs, combinatorics, collections, ciphers and codes, which then reveal just how rich and complicated are our communicative structures, in architecture and beyond.

CHAPTER 4

Indexical architecture

If you are new to C.S. Peirce you can be excused for finding it difficult to identify, remember, recall and operationalise Peirce's sign categories. Peirce admitted such difficulty, but considered that an asset.

> **It is a nice problem to say to what class a given sign belongs; since all the circumstances of the case have to be considered. But it is seldom requisite to be very accurate; for if one does not locate the sign precisely, one will easily come near enough to its character for any ordinary purpose of logic.**
> **(Peirce 1998e: 297)**

It is as if the process we go through to resolve difficult classifications provides some intellectual benefit. I have tried to argue that for an architectural scholar, Peirce's categories open architecture to multiple ways of thinking about meaning and significance, and otherwise unnoticed vehicles of communication, that is, to new *sign-vehicles* in architecture: not just architectural elements as sign-vehicles, but aspects of those elements. In his essay 'The Architectural Sign', Charles Jencks identified such communicative aspects as 'forms, spaces, surfaces, volumes which have suprasegmental properties (rhythm, colour, texture, density etc.)' and he added 'noise, smell, tactility, kinaesthetic quality, heat, etc.' (Jencks 1980: 73). This list of material and sensual attributes highlights another contribution of Peirce's seemingly arcane sign system: his emphasis on the concept of the index.

A return to the physical

The digital revolution in architecture as elsewhere brings many issues to the fore. Digital technology provides an exaggerated sense of the artificial and the virtual that in some quarters engenders their opposites: a respect for craft and pre-digital production, material qualities, physicality, the tactile, and an architecture responsive to the whole embodied sensorium, leading some commentators to declare this a 'post-digital' age. The idea of the post-digital accepts that the digital is still present; there is no escaping it. In writing about this post-digital condition, media commentator Florian Cramer identified a 'semiotic shift to the indexical' and away from symbols (Cramer 2015: 22). This insight about the indexical echoes that of art theorist Rosalind Krauss who noted a shift in art away from the symbolic.

> **As distinct from symbols, indexes establish their meaning along the axis of a physical relationship to their referents. They are the marks or traces of a particular cause, and that cause is the thing to which they refer, the object they signify. Into the category of the index, we would place physical traces (like footprints), medical symptoms, or the actual referents of the shifters. Cast shadows could also serve as the indexical signs of objects.**
>
> **(Krauss 1977: 70)**

She cites Marcel Duchamp's readymades, including a work called the *Large Glass*, in which elements 'are colored by the fixing of dust that had fallen on the prone surface of the glass over a period of months. The accumulation of dust is a kind of physical index for the passage of time' (Krauss 1977: 75). Peirce's emphasis on the indexical provides a means of elevating the role of the physical world in our communicative structures. The index points us back to the tangible and real, to footprints, shadows and dust.

As we have seen, according to Peirce, an indexical is a sign that refers to an object by being affected (or caused) by the object. The indexical relationship is a direct connection between a sign and its object, as if the sign is caused by its object (as smoke is caused by fire). Indexicality appeals to the post-digital as it diminishes the role of resemblances (icons) and abstractions (symbols). As affirmed by the semiotic scholar Felicia Kruse, the indexical sign has the potential to hold a more central role in the semiotic landscape than its 'more glamorous and elusive brethren, the icon and symbol' (Kruse 1986: 435). The index also moves attention away from expressive metaphors, which for Peirce were *icons* (Anderson 1984). Metaphorical signs do resemble other objects in some respects, as Jørn Utzon's Sydney Opera House resembles sails on the harbour, and Kengo Kuma's V&A museum in Dundee resembles the strata in a cliff face.

an indexical is a sign that refers to an object by being affected (or caused) by the object.

The low-key tenor of the indexical has currency in literature. In advising against writing florid prose, Mark Twain counselled writers to use adjectives and adverbs only sparingly (Schmidt 2018). Similarly, an *indexical architecture* depends less on being 'expressive', as either the purveyor (as sign) or the object of rich descriptive narrative. An indexical architecture avoids an architecture suffused with the spatial equivalents of colourful adverbs and adjectives. According to Peirce,

Figure 11 Pointing as an indexical sign.
Source: Author.

> The index asserts nothing; it only says 'There!' It takes hold of our eyes, as it were, and forcibly directs them to a particular object, and there it stops. Demonstrative and relative pronouns are nearly pure indices, because they denote things without describing them.
>
> (Peirce 1992d: 226)

Unembroidered facts circulate in the company of indexical signs. Forensic investigations in criminal cases inevitably appeal to the idea of the indexical sign: the bullet hole in the wall is a sign that someone fired a gun, as a fact. A crack in the wall is a sign of movement in the foundations. So, a 'shift to the indexical' implies that people are now inclined to give priority to effects and causes, and 'real' connections between the signs we use and the things we use them for, that is, the objects in the world.

Peirce did not provide a convenient monograph linking his theories together as a coherent system. So, others have had to take on this responsibility, and interpretations vary. In the rest of this chapter I will deliver my own understanding (with sources) linking Peirce's sign classifications with his understanding of logic and the implications for architectural design (Chapter 5).

Signs and facts

It is worth pursuing further the relationship between the indexical sign and the idea of a fact. Semiotic scholar Thomas Sebeok thought of the index as the most original and fruitful of Peirce's three classes of signs (the icon, index and symbol) (Sebeok 1999: 85). An indexical sign is a sign that derives from its object. Smoke is a sign of fire, because the smoke issues from the fire. We will even say the smoke is *caused* by the fire. Blood on the walls is an indexical sign of a violent struggle, as the bloodstain derives from the event, that is, an event involving the body of a victim under trauma. Lest we think that such ideas are removed from architecture, recall how Bernard Tschumi enigmatically aligned architecture with discourses about evidence, witnesses and murder (Tschumi 1994: 100): 'To really appreciate architecture, you may even need to commit a murder. Architecture is defined by the actions it witnesses as much as by the enclosure of its walls'.

In the case of an indexical sign there is some process that connects the object to the sign. Peirce said: 'An index stands for its object by virtue of a real connection with it' (Peirce 1998h: 14). You do not necessarily see the object that the sign connects to, but you see the indexical sign that has emerged from the object. Think of the condensation trail (contrail) left by a jet aircraft. You do not see the aeroplane, as it is too far away, or it has disappeared over the horizon, but the condensation trail tells you the plane is or was there. The contrail is an indexical sign of a jet-propelled aircraft.

The idea of the index is privileged in the realms of fact. An actual murder yields the sign of a bloodstain. An imaginary murder does not oblige us with the inevitable emergence of such a sign. You could say that imagination does not yield indexical signs. The object of an index is actual and factual – or at least that is the claim we make of it.

The idea of the index is privileged in the realms of fact.

Contrary to an indexical sign, as I showed in Chapter 3, an *icon* is a sign that resembles its object in some respects. A drawing of a murder is close to a pure icon of its object. A drawing does not derive from its object in the same way that an indexical sign derives from its object. A photograph is a different matter, however. A photograph or CCTV video of a murder taking place has more authority in a discussion about facts than a drawing, as the photograph does derive from the circumstances, the object, by virtue of some optical and mechanical processes, even if there is a risk the photograph or video is subsequently manipulated. Peirce assigned photographs to the class of indexicals, though there is also an iconic aspect to photographs (Peirce 1998d: 5–6). Photographs do 'resemble' their objects in certain respects visually.

Contrary to both an index and an icon, a symbolic sign functions differently in the ecology of facts. Apparently, the ruins of the ancient Mexican city of Monte Alban are marked with so-far undecipherable symbols (Heyworth 2014). The practices, places and rituals of that culture (as objects) do not cause or produce these obscure symbols, as if indices. Nor do they provide iconic signs that resemble their objects. Symbols do not have as secure a hold over their objects as do indexicals. Symbols are not so easily brought into service within discussions about facts.

But symbols are crucial within Peirce's schema. Symbols, by Peirce's definition, are cultural artefacts that conform to convention. All symbols are *legisigns*, forming systems with their own internal relational rules. There are many symbolic systems, including computer languages, road signs, emojis and astronomical signs. Spoken and written languages provide the most obvious day-to-day examples of symbolic sign systems. To refer back to Chapter 3, Peirce divides symbolic signs into words: [viii] *rhematic symbols*, ordinary propositions: [ix] *dicent symbols* and rules or arguments: [x] *arguments*.

The monumental architecture of Louis Kahn (1901–1973) was by most accounts sensitive to materials and context. He would famously ask of a building what it wants to be (Jencks and Kropf 1997: 236). But building elements do not speak back in words or other symbolic expressions. Objects do not deliver *symbolic* signs as if *indexicals*. A tree does not come with a ready-made label asserting 'I am a tree', as a symbolic sign. A column as object will not speak 'I am a column'. Notwithstanding moves towards an internet of electronically tagged things (Atzori et al. 2010) a column does not present symbols as if labels on a computer-aided design or BIM model. Nor will a murder weapon cry out 'I belong to the prime suspect'. Symbolic signs do not derive from their objects as indexicals do from theirs.

However, symbols (words, propositions and arguments) are essential currency in the world of facts. There are many ways of apprehending the world, but human linguistic practices deploy facts as statements in language. You do not look at a contrail in the sky and think 'fact' without some accompanying statement: for example, 'there is a plane up there'. Facts are statements in language, a language composed of symbols. Symbols carry the advantage that they can be linked, managed, inventoried and processed. Indexical signs are not so easily manipulated. But by most accounts, one of the hallmarks of being a rational human is that I can translate indexicals to symbols. We can speak about the world. Recall John Locke's words. We need signs of our ideas 'to communicate our thoughts to one another, as well as record them for our own use' (Locke 1976: 443). In Peirce's terminology, by *signs* Locke meant *symbolic* signs.

Translating indexical signs to symbols

To talk about an object–indexical relationship is to translate an indexical sign situation into a symbolic one. That renders the sign situation amenable to processing, manipulation and negotiation. After all, we do talk and write about indexical relationships: for example, 'look at those white streaks criss-crossing in the sky', 'dark red stains on the carpet are either blood or red wine', 'why are the awnings still up?' 'where there's smoke there's fire'.

Peirce's characterisation of the syllogism illustrates the relationship between an object and its indexical sign. In general terms, a syllogism that draws on indexicality looks something like this.

this is a particular object
this object produces a particular indexical sign
therefore, this indexical sign will appear.

As an architectural example consider a conversation in a building: 'I just pressed the lift button', 'if a person presses the button the lift arrives', 'therefore the lift will arrive'. Here is a less mechanical example germane to someone lighting a fire in a nineteenth-century apartment.

I have just lit a fire
fire produces smoke
therefore, smoke will appear.

The last line is a conclusion resulting from a logical deduction from a premise (I have just lit a fire) and a rule (fire produces smoke). Such statements need to be tightened up and expressed in more formal language, but even in this format, it is fair to say that logical deductions are uncontroversial. Whatever the validity of the first two lines of the syllogism, the third follows from them with some certainty.

But there are other ways of manipulating such statements, such as a process of *induction*. Induction is the production of a generalisation, a rule, derived from a statement about an object and an indexical sign.

this is a particular object
this sign appears
therefore, this object produces this sign.

An astute and rational observer of signs ought to wait till they have encountered several similar object–sign relationships before jumping to the generalisation as a conclusion. In the practical domain of keeping warm in an old apartment you might say:

this is a fire
smoke appears
therefore, fire produces smoke.

Several iterations of the fire-lighting episode, or advice from others who have similar experience with open fireplaces, produces a useful generalisation, and possible action, such as keeping the chimney clear of obstructions, so that any smoke produced disappears up the chimney without filling the room.

For the syllogism model, deduction and induction are common modes of inference. Deduction is certain; induction is risky and requires repeated observations of objects and indexes before you can generalise with any certainty. But Peirce introduced a third mode of inference within the syllogism: *abduction*. This is the term Peirce uses to characterise the process by which an observer concludes the presence of the object from the presence of a particular sign.

an indexical sign has appeared
this object will produce such an indexical sign
therefore, this object is present.

In the fireplace example:

smoke appears
fire produces smoke
therefore, there is a fire.

A prudent observer could be excused from approaching such a conclusion (the presence of an object from its supposed sign) with caution. There may be other candidate objects that produce the same sign. The smoke could come from smouldering ashes after a fire has ostensibly gone out. The sign may, in fact, be the smell of smoke from a neighbour's chimney. In other serious social contexts, history is replete with stories of misattributed causes, that is, the hasty identification of an object from indexical signs that are merely circumstantial, that is, borne of the particular circumstances and not as a general condition.

The quasi-logical process of *abduction* is obvious in the case of detective work, and observations of signs such as bloodstains. What happened, how, and who did it typically require the detective to gather up more signs that corroborate any of a number of candidate objects in the semiotic process. In such cases the signs are evidence. Outside of semiotic discourse the detective (or enthusiast following a case) might simply say they are looking for evidence.

Signs constitute evidence. That there is smoke is strong evidence of fire. That a weathervane is oriented to the east is strong evidence that the wind comes from that direction. 'Evidence' is a useful term, as it leaves room for error. Rarely does just a single sign provide a definite link to the underlying phenomenon (the object).

Signs work together to form bodies of evidence.

Figure 12 Smoke as an index of fire. Edinburgh Beltane Fire Festival.
Source: Author.

They contribute to confidence that something is, or will be, the case: the fire, the murder, the crime, the weather. Signs contribute to belief, which is the certainty or otherwise that we attach to an object, that is, as a symbolic proposition.

I hope that so far in this chapter I have established the strong link between Peirce's theory of signs and his theories about logical inference (deduction, induction and abduction). The idea of the index grounds the discussion of logic to the world of observation and experience. The link between signs and abduction resides in the priority Peirce gives to indexical signs, and the translation of indexicals to symbols, that is, to statements in language and logic. To reinforce Peirce's claims about abduction I want to turn to Peirce's concepts of inference more generally, as exercises in symbolic manipulation in ways that extend beyond the object–indexical relationship. In the process we learn something about architectural design, or at least how to position design and making within Peirce's schema. To do so I will re-visit the issue of abduction as interpretation in the next chapter.

Diagrammatic proof

So far, I have alluded to the manipulation of symbols, statements in language (e.g. 'fire produces smoke') as components of the syllogism, and as a means of

Figure 13 Peirce's simple diagrammatic proof that the two angles formed by a line that joins another along its length add up to two right angles (Peirce 1998l: 207). Source: Author.

deriving conclusions, generalisations and statements of fact. Peirce also deployed diagrams to explain such concepts. As iconic signs, diagrams are in the company of charts, graphs and tables, the authors of which extract the salient features of a phenomenon, show relationships and predict outcomes. Peirce was amongst the first to theorise the diagram. It is clear to me from the sparse collection of diagrams in his published papers that he was thinking mainly of diagrams in mathematical and geometrical proof. He wrote 'mathematical reasoning is diagrammatic' (Peirce 1998f: 206).

As a minimal illustration of the nature of the diagram he demonstrates the well-known geometrical proof that a line with an endpoint abutting another line forms two angles, the sum of which is equivalent to two right angles. See the diagrammatic proof above. The abutting line (sloping) creates two angles and defines a point on the second line (drawn horizontally here). By drawing a line perpendicular to the horizontal line, you see that there are two right angles. Therefore, the sum of the two angles formed by the abutting line equals two right angles.

This is arguably a trivial and unnecessary demonstration of a self-evident fact, though it has consequences in the derivation of proofs for more complicated and consequential geometries. When geometrical proofs were taught in schools I used to reach for my plastic protractor and measure the angles, and I would wonder why that simple induction was not sufficient to prove that the angles did what the theorems said. Peirce points out that for the diagrammatic proof to work the geometry student has to recognise that the diagram is not just about the lines as drawn, but signifies any two lines configured at any angle and of any length, colour, thickness, etc. The diagram is an *iconic legisign*. That we might take a diagram such as the line drawings that appeared in Chapter 3 and elsewhere to represent general conditions and not particular cases demonstrates for Peirce the mediated, relational, linguistic and learned characteristic of the diagram.

Peirce also had something to say about the diagrams of the mathematician John Venn (1834–1923), and others have had much to say about Peirce on diagrams (Leja 2000; Awbrey 2008; Shawcross 2012). Peirce developed his own system of logical diagrams that look superficially like Venn diagrams. He proposed a method for representing logical propositions diagrammatically, and in such a way that you can transform that diagram (through a series of rules) to demonstrate a logical proof. I will not take that approach any further in this book, but the importance of diagrams in logical proofs will be important in the next chapter.

CHAPTER 5

Abduction in architecture

It will be evident so far that Peirce was a systematiser and organiser of ideas. He considered himself a logician before he was a philosopher. As shown already in the previous chapter, logic uses symbolic signs. There is much in Peirce that speaks to mathematicians, systems theorists, digital practitioners and programmers in architecture. His yardstick was logic, which follows a method or a procedure to get from A to B, to transition from one sign to another, from evidence back to a cause, from a sign-vehicle to its object, a process that in general terms Peirce called 'semiosis' (Atkin 2016: 132). A method tells you what to do, as an ordered sequence. A method can also serve as an explanation of what happened or did not happen. The language philosopher Walter Ong, for example, maintained that the earliest use of method was as an aid to explain why a medical procedure was unsuccessful (Ong 1972). The idea of method also appears in early writing on architecture. For Vitruvius, *methodus* was a 'mode of proceeding' (OED), as in the case of constructing a building.

> The Greeks layout their forums in the form of a square surrounded by very spacious double colonnades, adorn them with columns set rather closely together, and with entablatures of stone or marble, and construct walks above in the upper story.
>
> (Vitruvius 1960: 132)

The method here advises the builder/architect to follow a template, a typology, as discussed in previous chapters, and construct the plan in a certain order.

Another term related to *method* here is *inference*. As I demonstrated in the previous chapter in relation to the object–indexical relationship, the model of inference on which Peirce drew is that of logical *deduction*. You start with a specific case and a general proposition and from those statements infer a new proposition, or conclusion. In semiotic terms these statements are *dicent symbols* (factual assertions) and *arguments* (generalisations or rules). In the previous chapter, I illustrated the syllogism via the direct link between an object and its indexical sign: if there is a fire then there will be smoke. Consider a further example involving classification.

If you accept that all mausoleums are buildings, and the Taj Mahal is a mausoleum, then you must conclude therefore that the Taj Mahal is a building. There are three propositions here:

The Taj Mahal is a mausoleum
All mausoleums are buildings
Therefore, the Taj Mahal is a building.

The first is a particular case. The second is a generalisation, or a rule. The third is a conclusion. You may disagree with the first two propositions, or not know whether they are true. But if you accept them as true then the third must follow as also true. This is a further example of Aristotle's syllogism: All men are mortal; Socrates was a man; Therefore, Socrates was mortal. The logical process is indifferent to the state of affairs in the world, that is, any indexical reference. It is a self-contained system dealing in propositional statements; and follows a method.

In this general case, a simple diagram (an *iconic legisign*) would prove the case: a circle that represents all buildings; a circle within that representing all mausoleums, and a dot within that inner circle representing the Taj Mahal. Clearly, the dot is in both the mausoleum circle and the building circle. If A is in B and B is in C, then A is also in C. The method here is simply to draw a diagram, substitute the propositional statements for the labels in the diagram and apply some simple set theory about containment. This method also constitutes a proof, that the statements are consistent with one another. Deduction can be much more complicated than this simple example illustrates, and deductions chain together. If A is true then B will follow, and B leads on to C, and D, and so on. The consequences for such a deductive inference may not be as obvious as the Taj Mahal example.

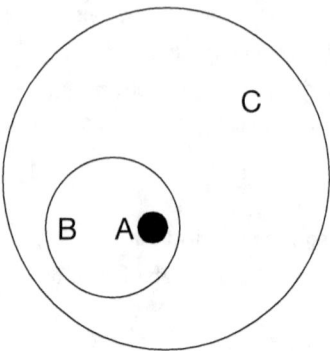

Figure 14 A simple Venn diagram illustrating the syllogism.
Source: Author.

In the 1980s, some of us worked with a programming language known as Prolog, for processing statements in logic, including statements that include variables (existential quantifiers) (Clocksin and Mellish 1981; Coyne 1988). An obvious application involved attempts to express supposed architectural rules, for example, building regulations as statements in predicate logic, and presume that the computer could make automatic inferences from such statements, that you could prove by logical deduction whether a building complied with the regulations. It is easy enough to replicate logical deductions in Prolog, though more difficult to codify rules and regulations as logic statements. For many reasons this is more difficult than we thought, but to follow such a method in this way is an example of logical *deduction*. It is a kind of inference that you can approach with some certainty. It assumes a certain outcome of true or false.

As I have shown, Peirce, amongst other logicians, also identified the process of *induction*. This is simply the establishment of a general rule from an instance. 'All mausoleums are buildings', is a generalisation, a rule that can be applied in many circumstances. If someone told (or showed) students of architecture that the Taj Mahal is a building, and also declared that it is a mausoleum, then they might infer that all mausoleums are buildings, but they could not be very certain of that fact from the information given. If you then showed them

Castel Sant'Angelo in Rome, the Pantheon in Paris and other buildings that are mausoleums, the outcome of the inductive inference gains strength. That is the nature of induction and its methods. Repeated observations help us to derive a general rule. Standard textbooks on the philosophy of science commonly identify this process as one of the main methods of science – deriving a general formula or rule from many experimental observations (Chalmers 1999). Induction is also the challenge of so-called 'machine learning': algorithms inspect lots of examples to infer by induction some generalisations (Barr et al. 1981).

Peirce's third type of inference, *abduction*, is a process whereby you start with a generalisation, that all mausoleums are buildings, and an assertion that the Taj Mahal is a building, and conclude that therefore the Taj Mahal is a mausoleum. You cannot, by the deductive method outlined above, form that conclusion. At best you could characterise the conclusion as a guess rather than a deduction. There is nothing in the statements 'All mausoleums are buildings', and 'The Taj Mahal is a building' that would lead you with any certainty to the view that the Taj Mahal is a mausoleum. The building you are considering could be a restaurant, a hotel, a house or a bike shed. There is evidence in the statements that I am thinking about mausoleums, as I've just made reference to that building type, but no certainty from the logic of the statements. Further evidence could come from familiarity with famous exemplars of building types, and the context of the discussion – a lecture or book on architecture, not to mention a photograph of the building and other indexical signs. Evidence will also come filtered by our predispositions, biases and affinities with certain kinds of buildings.

Peirce's strong argument on logic is that abduction is the most usual and typical kind of inference. Sometimes it is called 'uncertain inference', or 'evidential reasoning'. As I indicated in Chapter 4, abduction helps explain how indexical signs function as evidence.

Peirce's strong argument on logic is that abduction is the most usual and typical kind of inference

Abduction in the smart city

To bring Peirce's thinking up to date with an architectural and urban example, consider the processing of urban data. Peirce's concept of abduction is relevant to the notion of the contemporary smart city (Picon 2015; Willis and Aurigi 2018). Supposed 'smart cities' do not only trade in intellectual capital, but they collect and process data from widely distributed networks of sensors that pick up traffic flows, environmental conditions, and human activity to perform calculations, that in turn regulate flows in the city. The obvious example is an integrated transportation system that responds intelligently to fluctuations in demand. The more controversial and interesting application of such big data processing is the use of personal and private transactions, as individuals leave digital traces of their commercial activity and as people communicate with one another. Much of this digital surveillance is now available to people and organisations with the knowhow. Social media platforms lay bare the opportunities and risks of such big data analytics (Kitchin 2014).

Peirce's concept of abduction is relevant to the notion of the contemporary smart city

Can you infer and map people's needs, preferences and politics from their online footprint? Consider a person's preferences for outdoor activities and being in nature settings. If you were raised in a school and home environment that encouraged you to spend time outdoors and enjoy nature pursuits, then it is likely that in later life you will favour recyclable products, consider energy efficiency, enjoy being out in nature settings, desire access to a garden, and even enjoy looking at pictures of nature scenes. Call those early life experiences A, and behaviours and attitude in later life B. In this case there is popular and research literature connecting A to B in a causal way. Early life experiences A (as objects) generate indexical signs B. In most cases people would accept that A implies B. A certain upbringing produces particular observable or reportable life habits. You could draw such inferences by logical deduction, or at least they are inferences you could make with some certainty.

Now reverse the logic. You meet someone who talks a lot about the environment, likes outdoor pursuits and enjoys nature scenes. You might conclude that in early life they were raised in a nature-loving environment and as a child spent a lot of time outdoors. But you will be less sure of that. The causal links here become frayed. After all, someone could have had a nature epiphany in later life, decided to catch up on what they missed as a child, or yielded to the enthusiasms of a newly found nature-loving social circle. So, there is considerable uncertainty in this case in thinking that B implies A. But in so far as we attempt that inference, it comes under the category of logical *abduction*. Certainty is low in such reasoning, and you would need more information to conclude something about a person's upbringing, especially if you are not able to ask them directly.

To find out about an adult person's childhood, you could examine their recent social media activity on Facebook, Instagram or Twitter, and see how often they talk about, like, re-post or show pictures of outdoor pursuits, link to environmental causes, and even post pictures of nature settings. That would at least establish the B part of the logical equation. You may be able to find other evidence that hints at the kind of upbringing they had: anecdotes, advice, attitudes to children, etc. That would help establish the A part. Now think of just one part of the B equation, for example, preference for looking at, re-posting, or linking to pictures of nature. You could reasonably deduce (by looking at or using an algorithm) from a person's Facebook feed that they like nature pictures, more than pictures of cars, people or buildings. Could you (or an algorithm) then infer (by abduction) something about the person's upbringing? With the right detective skills, you probably could. The challenge posed by the sharing of personal data is not simply the data itself but what can be inferred about you (by abduction) from it, especially when inspected in the context of a large number of other participants. The University of Cambridge Psychometrics Centre provides an online demonstration that claims to accurately predict 'psychological traits from digital footprints of human behaviour', taking Facebook posts, Twitter feeds or authored texts as input (Popov et al. 2018).

That is one of the intriguing and disturbing aspects of online personal information. Our digital footprint reveals more about us than we state explicitly, and some of it can be gleaned from simple data like our choices of images. It will not just help an investigator infer whether a person had a nature-loving upbringing, but something about their schooling, educational attainment, ethnic background, social circle, disposable income, purchasing habits, the kinds of holidays they take, alcohol consumption, and personality profile. Such data can be processed in the aggregate to inform decision-making in the day-to-day and long-term organisation of the smart city.

The methods deployed involve machine learning, probabilistic inference and statistical analysis from very large numbers of observations, examples or cases. Automated abduction across large sectors of a population is not necessarily accurate, but it does not have to be. It is the aggregation of such assessments that can inform city processes. Online targeted marketing also makes use of this kind of abductive inference and, if automated, it only has to be approximately correct about any individual's position within a demographic to impact large groups of people, and hence have an effect on persuasion, politics, place and profits. People mostly understand the way logical deduction works, but abduction is less intuitive as a concept, and less well understood. There are benefits and risks from assuming the ability to infer undeclared facts from databases of evidence. Peirce's concepts of abduction help us understand such processes.

Forensic architecture

Concepts of evidence inform architecture in other ways as well. The idea of evidence is obviously important in a juridical context. Evidence comes to the fore when architects deal with compliance (codes and regulations), and get caught up in legal matters, such as contract disputes, liability and compensation claims, and as witnesses. Evidence is also important in any kind of research context, as when we draw on evidence to support a hypothesis, or to support a judgement, or any interpretation.

Within Peirce's sign classification system, the role of iconic signs for architecture is clear. Any architect would also appreciate the role of symbols in architecture. I titled the previous chapter 'Indexical architecture'. But what constitutes an indexical architecture is an open question. As I have shown, an indexical sign has the characteristic that it emanates from its object, as if caused by it. It is a direct relationship requiring no mediating concept, that is, none of the entailments of a resemblance (icon) or convention (symbol). You could say that an index is a cognitively vacuous sign – perhaps a mute or primitive sign, like a pointing finger. There are four approaches to architecture that are candidates for the idea of an indexical architecture.

First, an indexical architecture depends less on being 'expressive', as either the purveyor (as sign) or object of rich descriptive narrative, that is, an architecture drenched in theory, meaning, metaphor or ornament, of adverbs and adjectives. An indexical architecture therefore speaks to that branch of twentieth-century architectural modernism that goes under the heading of *functionalism*. An article by Claire Zimmerman demonstrates how the history of architectural modernism presents variations on the concept of the index, particularly in relation to the indexical character of photography (Zimmerman 2012). Similar to the truth claims of a photograph, a functionalist building attempts to demonstrate truthfully what it is in its construction, form and use of materials.

> We might call a building 'demonstrative' if it shows us its own construction (in process and in final result), how it is to be occupied, and how it may have created meaning for its users. 'Indexical' implies something else in addition, by suggesting that there may be truth value to the demonstration – akin to the 'truth' established by a footprint or a thumbprint as evidence of the prior presence of a foot or a thumb.
>
> (2012: 277)

In discussing James Stirling's Leicester Engineering Building, she suggested that the architect anticipated the building's photographic representation, and designed it to be legible as a series of images: 'It is explicit about its own manufacture' (2012: 279). She drew on Peirce for her definition of the index. In summary, 'Architectural indexicality can be located as an idea in nineteenth-century structural rationalism and discourses around twentieth-century functionalism' (2012: 277).

Second, an indexical architecture references an architecture of movement, and hence participation. In an article appropriately titled 'An indexical approach to architecture', Anne Bordeleau wrote, 'The fact that the index is embedded in the very materiality of the world makes it particularly appealing to the consideration of architecture' (Bordeleau 2008: 86). This led her to think of a participatory architecture that you move through and engage with. She drew on the indexical metaphor of pointing. To know what is being pointed at in a space you need to be familiar with it, a condition abetted by moving through that space. She added, 'to approach architecture indexically is to root comprehension in participation' (2008: 88). By this reading, an indexical architecture is an architecture of engagement rather than expression. It is also an architecture of direct visceral response.

Third, contrary to such a human-centred approach, and in keeping with the idea of the 'smart city', I think of architecture that deploys sensing devices and actuators to control the environment in response to the changing conditions of the occupants and the weather, as also indexical. Algorithms and code have a part to play in the configuration of surface and space. The photosensitive panels in a building facade that turn into shading elements provide indexical signs that the sun is bright, fulfilling the requirements of a so-called responsive architecture (Beesley et al. 2006). In this case the building operates as a sign in a way similar to the indexical function of the weathervane.

A further response to the challenge of an indexical architecture comes under the heading of 'forensic architecture', as developed by Eyal Weizman and his team (Weizman 2017). They gathered evidence in support of cases that have a spatial aspect. Weizman began his book *Forensic Architecture* with an account of a legal trial that involved the minute examination of an Auschwitz death chamber. He maintained that their work 'demonstrates the ongoing tension between testimony and evidence – material and linguistic practices, subject and object and the complex interdependencies between violence and the negation of evidence that are central to the field of forensic architecture' (2017: 20).

The Forensic Architecture web site (Weizman 2018) is rich with projects and examples. They do not seem to reference Peirce or indexicality in their discourse, but the theme of evidence looms large. In an account of their exhibition, they see their work as 'a form of investigative practice that traverses architectural, journalistic, legal and political fields, and moves from theoretical examination to practical application'. Digital and sensing technologies play a major role in their investigations. This is not pure detective work however, but an ethos that

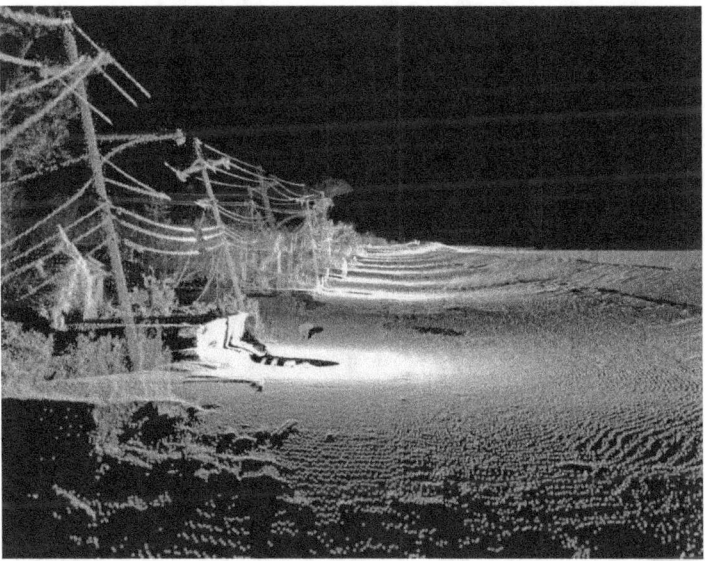

Figure 15 Evidence of an urban catastrophe. Composite LiDAR scan of New Orleans after Hurricane Katrina in August 2005.
Source: Still image from a cinematic installation by Asad Khan (Khan 2018).

imbues their work. An exhibition at the London ICA gallery indicated their use of satellite imagery and data sharing, material analysis, digital reconstructions, and included 'elements of witness testimony and the cumulative forms of visual documentation enabled by contemporary media' (Weizman et al. 2018).

Indexicality (under the theme of evidence) becomes a focus of architectural practice. It also informs an approach to design and presentation: an inaesthetic, evidential approach to architecture. As lawyers are apt to say if the thing speaks for itself – *res ipsa loquitur*.

Indefinite inference

It is worth testing Peirce's account of abduction against the tenets of hermeneutics. Outside of automated abduction, from a hermeneutical perspective we are always in an uncertain condition. How you interpret, understand and act, depends on circumstances, which in turn draw on your background, history, the company you keep, the sense of your community (common sense), values, beliefs, habits, practices, the material circumstances of the moment, and of course the advice of others. How we interpret, understand and act may be embedded in our practices without reflection, or they can be the subject of a concerted process of decision-making, hesitation, debate and dispute with or without resolution. For hermeneutical scholars such as Hans-Georg Gadamer (1900–2001), to interpret, to understand and to act (apply our understanding) is the same process (Gadamer 1975). To understand a situation is to act in it. If there are stated rules and norms, then their application is also contingent, a matter of interpretation.

For the hermeneutical scholar formal logic rarely comes into play or decides the matter, or, at least, logical deduction is rare, where one proposition follows another in an inevitable chain of inference. For Peirce, reasoning was mostly abduction, a reverse process of inference by which we try to create the situation about which inferences could be made to deduce a conclusion – a conclusion that we propose ahead of time.

As we have seen, Peirce asserted the primary role of abduction in human reasoning. The ubiquity of abduction fits the hermeneutical model, as long as we do not feel the need to adhere to formal logic (as does Peirce) in defining what it is to reason, judge and think. Indeed, for Peirce, we exhibit abductive judgements via a range of processes; not least in the sudden flash of an understanding (a 'hunch') that is the result of an informal process.

> The abductive suggestion comes to us like a flash. It is an act of insight, although of extremely fallible insight. It is true that the different elements of the hypothesis were in our minds before; but it is the idea of putting together what we had never before dreamed of putting together which flashes the new suggestion before our contemplation.
>
> (Peirce 1998i: 227)

The ubiquity of abduction fits the hermeneutical model, as long as we do not feel the need to adhere to formal logic (as does Peirce) in defining what it is to reason, judge and think.

He added that this kind of abduction is 'a process not sufficiently conscious to be controlled' (1998i: 227). He declared that if we were to subject this abductive process to logical analysis then we would have to accept that it follows a chain of inference that never ends. In fact, he said it is an indefinite process 'because it is subconscious and so not amenable to logical criticism, does not have to make separate acts of inference but performs its act on one continuous process' (1998i: 227).

The instantaneity of such sudden (abductive) insight testifies that something is going on other than formal logic. That is not to trivialise or mystify such apparently instantaneous processes. We interpret, judge, decide, act from moment to moment, and all the time. For the purposes of argument, I am content to match Peirce's concept of abduction with hermeneutical concepts of interpretation.

I am content to match Peirce's concept of abduction with hermeneutical concepts of interpretation.

Conceding to Peirce the centrality of semiotics, abductive reasoning inevitably brings signs into play, as we gather evidence during the thought process, in conversation or in retrospect as we justify our interpretations, understandings and actions. A helpful online article by Gary Shank and Donald Cunningham outlined several modes of abduction consistent with Peirce's categories of the sign (Shank and Cunningham 1996). They used the term 'evidence' throughout. Signs go to make up the evidence that informs an abductive inference.

To paraphrase the first part of their article, abductive interpreters can follow a hunch (or make a guess), taking their own unarticulated feelings about a case as evidence. This is a qualitative assessment with little apparent ground. It is a raw and poorly articulated feeling, as described above. But in abduction we can also follow the evidence of a symptom; or move from one frame of reference to another via analogy or metaphor; we can pick up clues, as does the investigator of a crime; we can formulate a diagnosis compiled as a set of clues; and/or we can follow the route of ascertaining facts on the basis of how they can be woven into a plausible narrative or explanation.

Shank and Cunningham reviewed these modes of abduction, or sources of evidence, in relation to Peirce's ten sign classification system. Deduction seems to pertain to the notion of argument – number [x] on Peirce's ten classes of signs identified in Chapter 3. This is the evidence gleaned from strict logical inference. Induction pertains to the notion of the *dicent* [iv, vii, ix], a complete qualitative expression (e.g. fire produces smoke, all mausoleums are buildings, all men are mortal). Abduction belongs to the *rheme*, which is an 'open propositional function' according to Shank and Cunningham. Most types of sign with which Peirce is concerned fall into this category.

Design as abduction

Architecture presents the even more radical idea that buildings come about by processes of abduction. To build is to manufacture something about which evidence can be derived. A building or component is an object from which critics, evaluators and users might derive evidence. In this sense, to design something is to start with a statement about the evidence you would like to have, and work by abductive inference back to an object that would deliver that evidence.

By this reading, this pre-determined evidence constitutes a propositional statement, a proposal, a goal, an aim, a programme or a brief. The designed object is created *ex post-facto* to fit the evidence. The act of designing has been usefully defined as an abductive process leading from some putative evidence (e.g. qualities and desirable characteristics) backwards to the object that would provide that evidence. It is as if the architect is constructing a crime scene in reverse, about which others have already picked up evidence (signs) and made observations and judgements. As for any project, the brief for the V&A museum at Dundee illustrated in Chapter 2 provided such *ex post-facto* evidence: the building will 'be a rich and inspiring resource for design and creativity; attract visitors from Dundee, Scotland and further afield to world-class travelling and permanent exhibitions; improve the attractiveness of Dundee and its region to business' (Turner 2010). Whether or not the completed building ultimately provides such 'evidence', a design so directed follows a Peircean, abductive process. Or, at least, Peirce's theory of abduction provides a viable account of the relationship of design to logic.

The act of designing has been usefully defined as an abductive process leading from some putative evidence (e.g. qualities and desirable characteristics) backwards to the object that would provide that evidence.

Abduction as a mode of architectural inference entered the design lexicon via the work of the mathematician and pioneer of computer-aided architecture Lionel March (1934–2018). He presented the concept of abduction in the introduction to his edited book *The Architecture of Form* in which he examined Peirce's concepts of induction, deduction and abduction (March 1976). The early Design Methods Movement advocated that design should proceed in an inevitable manner from information about a design problem to a design solution (Alexander 1964). March argued against the naïve proposition that the design of a building is a simple deductive process, that all we need is the full range of facts pertinent to the design challenge, and that design can and should proceed in a purely methodical way. He recruited Peirce's theory to argue that this is not the case. March thought abduction provides a suitable account of the design process as it indicates the contingency of design outcomes. March characterised this challenge as a matter of *value*. People bring competing values to the design process, as they bring competing insights to the process of abduction.

It turns out that Peirce's ideas about logic show the limits of logic, but also suggest how ideas from formal logic can be recruited in design. To reiterate, March cautioned against confidence in systematised design methods, positioning design in the uncertain but productive mode of abductive inference – inventing the cases about which deductions can be made. I was struck by March's use, in passing, of the evocative term 'shadow of doubt' to identify the black remnants in his inference diagrams, redrawn here from his article. They also bring to mind Krauss's suggestion about the indexicality of shadows (Krauss 1977), and the writer Junichiro Tanizaki's evocative essay on dark and indeterminate architectural recesses (Tanizaki 1977).

March's circular diagrams are arranged in three columns that provide permutations of the elements of the syllogism.

x is in y
y is in z
therefore x is in z.

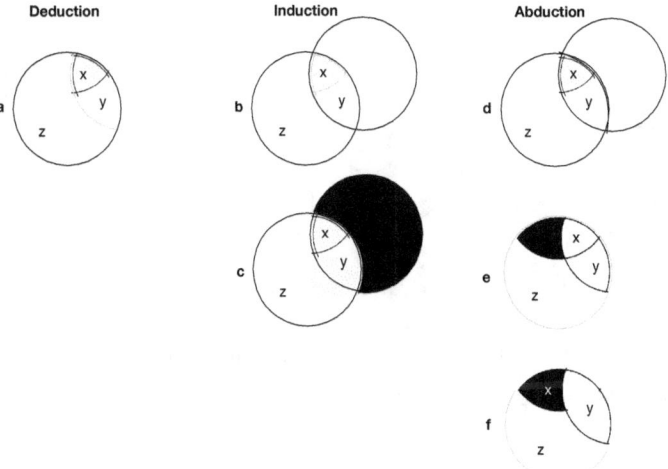

Figure 16 Permutations of the elements of the syllogism, after March (1976: 17). Source: Author.

If this seems too abstract then you can substitute the terms I used earlier to help explain the syllogism.

The Taj Mahal is a mausoleum
All mausoleums are buildings
Therefore, the Taj Mahal is a building.

In March's diagram, the top row of fragments of three intersecting circles (a, b, d) shows the condition we would like to assert with confidence, if only we could. The cases c, e and f indicate the degree to which the support for the condition in the top row is lacking – which he labelled suggestively 'the shadows of doubt'. Here is March's caption to the diagram (his figure 5 on page 17). I have adjusted the labels to the six circular diagrams (a–f), and I have changed his use of 'x ≤ y' etc. to 'x is in y' (all in square brackets []).

> Peirce's three modes of inference. There is one form of analytic reasoning, the deductive, shown in [a] as logically determined. There are two forms of

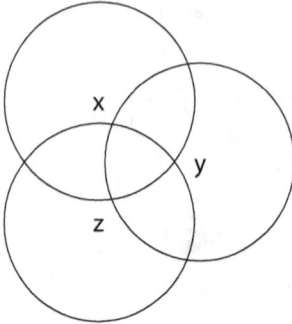

Figure 17 The three conditions and their relationships from which the circular segments in March's diagram are derived.
Source: Author.

synthetic reasoning, the inductive and the productive [i.e. abductive]. The hope in inductive reasoning is to arrive at the conclusion shown in [b]. However, there is no logical necessity for this and the typical outcome must look like [c] where the black part of [y] indicates the amount by which the rule [y is in z] is not met. Abductive reasoning has three distinct possibilities. In [d], as in the ideal world of Sherlock Holmes, the motive (rule) and the evidence (results) conspire 'beyond all reasonable doubt' – but without logical certainty – to prove the accused guilty (case). In [e], more typically, there is a shadow of doubt marked by the black part of [x] suggesting the degree by which [x is in y] is not supported. [f] is yet another possibility. Here the evidence and the motive simply do not tie up: [x], the black zone, is disjoint from [y].

Example f indicates: knowing that a mausoleum (y) is a building (z), and that the Taj Mahal is not a mausoleum (x) (e.g. perhaps it is a restaurant or some other type) negates the possibility that the Taj Mahal is a mausoleum. It may also help to recognise that the diagrams are derived from three intersecting circles containing all possible common areas, as shown above.

These diagrams are ostensibly about classification and may seem removed from the processes of designing buildings, for example, designing the Taj Mahal.

March's argument operates by analogy. Abduction encapsulates the difficult, iterative and indeterminate process by which you discover or invent a case that satisfies some evidence. Note March's use of the term 'evidence'. It also encapsulates the iterative and open-ended processes of design. March's account of design positions abduction within the canon of architectural thinking, and there are many scholars who pursue its application within design (Dorst 2011; Koskela et al. 2017). March's reflection also serves as a reminder of the power of diagrams (icons), and the open-ended nature of interpretation.

Abduction versus interpretation

I have already alluded to the similarities between Peirce's concept of abduction and the process of interpretation, called 'hermeneutics', as discussed by Gadamer. Nöth's *Handbook of Semiotics* has a chapter on hermeneutics, which contains a cogent account of the similarity between Peirce's description of abductive inference and Gadamer's hermeneutics.

> For [...] hermeneutics, textual understanding (and human knowledge in general) is possible neither by induction, i.e., by beginning with the textual (or experiential) data and arriving at a general explanation of the text (or law, concerning other phenomena) as a whole, nor by deduction, i.e., by beginning with a general law or knowledge of the whole and explaining the data through it. Against these unidirectional models of scientific discovery, the hermeneutics [sic] propose an alternative model of understanding, not unrelated to the alternative which Peirce introduced under the designation of abduction, the method of explaining data on the basis of assumptions and hypotheses about probable, not yet certain laws.
> (Nöth 1990: 336)

Others have thought along these lines, notably Peirce scholars Roland Daub-Schackat (1996) and Ines Riemer (1996). They described abduction as an iterative process. To abduct is to interpret. As an interpreter you start the process with some kind of hypothesis, a series of propositions about the meaning or value of the thing you are interpreting (e.g. a building, a film, a book, a blog or an utterance). Then you subject that hypothesis to testing and revision in light of the encounter. You revise the hypothesised meaning, and you do so repeatedly. For Reimer, 'The three step [sic] consisting of abduction, deduction and induction forms a cyclical or iterative process' (Riemer 1996: 393).

Under the abductive model, this repetitive movement, and what comes out of it, makes up what it is to understand a text, a building or a design. Such a process is ongoing, and is settled only provisionally, or to some pragmatic end. You do not stop when you alight on a moment of truth, as if an absolute. As circumstances change and different evidence comes to light then new interpretations emerge.

As in the arts and humanities, such processes permeate the sciences. This abductive process is iterative and circular, or some would say a series of nested or overlaid spirals or helixes. It is the hermeneutical circle. There are similarities between processes of abduction and the hermeneutical circle, but there are also differences. To my mind, the main difference is the way Peirce's account begins with the idea of a hypothesis.

The abductive model of what constitutes a hypothesis is the proposition – a [viii] rhematic symbol, a [ix] dicent symbol or an [x] argument – a statement in language ready for processing in logic, ill-formed and provisional, but a statement in logic nonetheless. For Peirce, the question of interpretation comes back to logical deduction as the final arbiter of truth and validity. I think Peirce loosens this connection with logic in some of his writing, but once logical deduction is set as the benchmark it is then very difficult to get away from its hold over reason.

Gadamer, on the other hand, writing from the perspective of the human sciences (i.e. the humanities), posited no such starting point in logic. His approach unshackles interpretation from logic, and it invokes a rich field of explanation and metaphor. I have outlined some of these metaphors elsewhere, notably in the book with Adrian Snodgrass: *Interpretation in Architecture*

(Snodgrass and Coyne 2006). Rather than a hypothesis, the interpreter comes to the task from a background of experience that contributes a pre-understanding, a fore-projection (or even a prejudice) that undergoes revision in light of the interpretative situation. It is hard to pin such a fore project down to a series of hypotheses. Nor is it the case that the interpreter verifies propositional speculations via the certainty of logical deduction.

Riemer referred to a cyclical process of 'abduction, deduction and induction'. I would say that interpretation is a cyclical process of repeated interpretations. The hermeneutical circle is interpretation all the way through. One reason Gadamer said that interpretation has ontological significance is that interpreters undergo transformation as they interpret. Peirce said that 'man is a sign' (Peirce 1992g: 54). Gadamer might have said that people are constituted by their prejudices. As people become open to the possibilities of interpretation they, and their pre-understandings, are also open to transformation.

CHAPTER 6

Nature semiotics

I have already shown how Peirce's logic puts the focus on indexical signs, that is, the signs that derive directly from their objects. Amongst other insights, Peirce's philosophy connects signs with the natural world. The semiotician and linguist Thomas Sebeok (1920–2001) extended Peirce's theory of signs to what he terms *biosemiotics*. For Sebeok, the theory of semiotics begins with living things. The minimal semiotic unit is the living cell found in the small and the large, the simple and the complicated, microorganisms and human beings. Sebeok thought of human bodies as 'assemblages of cells, about one hundred thousand billion (10^{14}) of them, harmoniously attuned to one another by an incessant flux of vital messages' (Sebeok 1999: 28). Organic systems circulate signs by many means, ranging from the exchange and transmission of genetic code between generations, to hormones and neurotransmitters within organisms: 'a variety of non-verbal and verbal messages conjoin organisms into a network of relations with each other as well as with the rest of their environment' (Sebeok 1999: 28–9). For biosemiotics, nature is one whole interconnected system, united through a network of signs.

<u>The minimal semiotic unit is the living cell found in the small and the large, the simple and the complicated, microorganisms and human beings.</u>

It is worth noting that architecture has a stake in the interconnected unity of nature, an ideal manifested not least as a putative harmony within nature and between human beings and nature. Alberto Perez-Gomez has written that at its best, architecture connects with 'integrity, wholeness, and holiness', an aspect of our world all but lost in the modern age (Perez-Gomez 2016: 90). Though of a different philosophical persuasion, the design theorist Christopher Alexander asserted something similar.

> **This is a fundamental view of the world. It says that when you build a thing you cannot merely build that thing in isolation, but must also repair the world around it, and within it, so that the larger world at that one place becomes more coherent, and more whole; and the thing which you make takes place in the web of nature, as you make it.**
>
> (Alexander et al. 1977: xiii)

Peirce's naturalist philosophy similarly advocated such harmony with nature (Houser 1998: xxxii). Much of Peirce's nature philosophy builds on the idea of oneness (Peirce 1998b), a view that there is one substance, an interconnected unity, a philosophy manifested in its various flavours as *monist* (Botar 2016). Semiotics at times reads as a departure from such interconnected unities, as if individuating, inspecting and classifying biological or other natural specimens. After all, semiotics orders families, genera, species, and subspecies of signs. Peirce's enthusiastic recourse to classificatory subdivisions is not entirely inconsistent with his holism, especially if classification is seen as a pragmatic tool that we adapt according to needs. In any case, Peirce's broad system of signs helps wrest nature from human language as master metaphor, as if nature must always give way to human cultural formations.

Nature's signs

Much discourse on architecture and nature has focused on the imitation of nature, as in the case of Laugier's story about how early architecture imitated the arrangement of four tree trunks as a rustic hut (Laugier 1977), one of architecture's origin myths. Durand titled his discussion of architecture 'From Imitation of Nature to Utility' (Durand 2000: 31). Note also the more recent development of biomimetic architectures, enhanced by advanced digital modelling (Gruber 2011; Armstrong 2015).

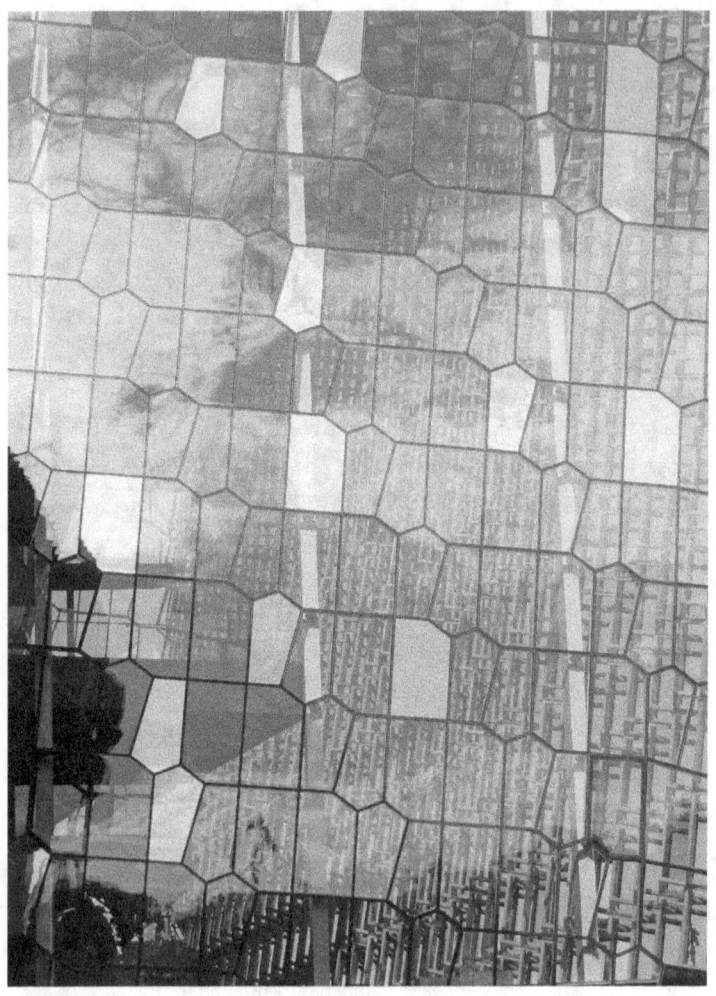

Figure 18 Organic architecture. Reykjavík, Iceland. Harpa Concert Hall and Conference Centre, Henning Larsen Architects.
Source: Author.

Imitation is of course a semiotic function addressed through the idea of the icon. Reiterating Peirce, Sebeok affirmed the character of an icon with examples from the animal world. Some insects emit an alarm signal via a chemical, the intensity of which mirrors the intensity of the threat: 'The sign is iconic inasmuch as it varies in analogous proportion to the waxing or waning of the danger stimuli' (Sebeok 1999: 52). He also referred to insects that mimic other more dangerous species, such as wasps, to deceive birds that prey on them. Icons mimic the object being referenced, and in this respect such insects use their bodies as *iconic* signs (Sebeok 1999: 84).

Sebeok also provided a naturalistic account of the *index*. The index operates via a direct relationship. So, nature is replete with indexical signs:

> **Signs, inclusive of indexes, occur at their most primitive on the single-cell level, as physical or chemical entities, external or internal with respect to the embedding organism as a reference frame, which they may 'point' to, read, or microsemiotically parse – in brief, can issue functional instructions for in the manner of an index.**
>
> (Sebeok 1999: 90–1)

Figure 19 Simulated fossilised organic entities by Asad Khan and Patricia Wu Wu. (Khan and Wu Wu 2017).
Source: Asad Khan (used with permission).

The indexicality of nature is also apparent as human beings impose themselves into the world. Sebeok invoked the idea of 'the book of nature' as dealing in indexical signs (Sebeok 1999: 94), for example, following animal trails in the hunt and reading animal entrails to tell the future (divination) (Sebeok 1999: 94), as if nature is written in a kind of code (Sebeok 1999: 96).

Sebeok also addressed 'natural' *symbols*. We might think that only human beings generate and read symbols, but Sebeok argued that 'the capacity of organisms to form intentional class concepts obtains far down in phylogenesis' (Sebeok 1999: 58). He refers to animal behaviours that seem unconnected with any function, such as when a dog wags its tail. Consider also bower birds that collect brightly coloured objects to attract a mate, and the species of fly (*Empididae*) that forms balloon shapes from its secretions with which it tries to impress a potential mate. Such gestures and objects appear useless, except for how they function as symbolic signs amongst human and non-human animals and organisms.

Pansemiotics

Peirce's semiotic naturalism culminated in his assertions about *pansemiotics*. Peirce claimed of semiotics that it is a universal science, covering fields known to Peirce in the nineteenth century, such as mathematics, ethics, metaphysics, gravitation, thermodynamics, optics, chemistry, comparative anatomy, astronomy, psychology, phonetics, economics, the history of science, play, wine and the human condition. But pansemiotics also expands the claims of semiotics beyond how human beings interpret the world. It subsumes humankind as a participant in semiotic processes, rather than a controller, interpreter or generator of signs. Nöth described Peirce's 'pansemiotic view of the universe' thus.

> **The point of departure of Peirce's theory of signs is the axiom that cognition, thought, and even man are semiotic in their essence. Like a sign, a thought refers to other thoughts and to objects of the world so that 'all which is reflected upon has [a] past'.**
>
> (Nöth 1990: 41)

But pansemiotics also expands the claims of semiotics beyond how human beings interpret the world. It subsumes humankind as a participant in semiotic processes, rather than a controller, interpreter or generator of signs.

His last quote is from Peirce's article 'Questions Concerning Certain Faculties Claimed for Man' (Peirce 1992f: 24). Nöth drew attention to Peirce's proposition that every thought is a sign, and life is a train of thought (Nöth 1990: 41). Peirce asserted 'that all this universe is perfused with signs, if it is not composed exclusively of signs' (Peirce 1998j: 394). That signs are so pervasive in nature, led Peirce to assert boldly that we human beings are signs.

> For, as the fact that every thought is a sign, taken in conjunction with the fact that life is a train of thought, proves that man is a sign; so, that every thought is an external sign, proves that man is an external sign. That is to say, the man and the external sign are identical, in the same sense in which the words homo and man are identical. Thus my language is the sum total of myself; for the man is the thought.
>
> (Peirce 1992g: 54)

That signs are so pervasive in nature, led Peirce to assert boldly that we human beings are signs.

Pansemiotics is here stated in anthropocentric terms, but it does not take much of a stretch to think that communication is going on whether we human beings are part of it or not.

Pansemiotics has not yet made it into the Oxford English Dictionary. The term crops up several times in Nöth's *Handbook of Semiotics*. The term translates the theological view that 'the whole universe became [in the Middle Ages] signs of divine revelation' (Nöth 1990: 382), as in the Old Testament statement, 'The heavens declare the glory of God' (Psalm 19:1), as if everything in the universe is united in this primary mission to communicate divine glory. By another reading, according to Nöth, 'any information processing by individual organisms (but not by machines) constitutes an instance of communication' (Nöth 1990: 170). Anything that involves information exchange (the transmission of signals between cells and organs, genetic exchange, etc.) constitutes a semiotic system. In summarising Peirce's contribution to pansemiotics, Nöth notes: 'In a pansemiotic perspective, communication is any form of semiosis' (Nöth 1990: 170).

Geosemiotics

One might readily accept that living systems operate semiotically, but what of the inorganic? Peirce may have had geological processes in mind as he constructed his theories of semiotics. He was a geologist, and he made his living in the U.S. Coast Survey. The geologist Victor R. Baker expanded on Peirce's philosophy to show how signs operate within geology. Baker laid out the basis of *geosemiotics*, advancing the strong Peircean thesis that semiotic processes continue 'from the natural world to the thought processes of geological investigators' (Baker 1999: 633). Peirce's classification of signs certainly applies to the practices of geologists. Drawings, maps and scans could be iconic signs. A rock sample as an indexical sign will divulge some process to which its appearance is linked causally. Like all scientists, geologists use symbols (Baker 1999: 638). Geologists and other human interpreters use and read inorganic signs. But how is the ecology of signs evident within geological systems independent of human presence?

Baker's geosemiotics supports the view that all of nature consists of webs of sign systems independent of human agency. Human beings merely participate in these webs from time to time. We are part of 'a semiotic web, according to which things and objects interweave to make up the fabric of experience' (Baker 1999: 641). It is as if experience and thinking reside in the larger environment, rather than something introduced into it by human beings. For

Baker, the ways geologists process information 'constitute sign relationships that extend continuously from the physical world of what is observed to the mental world that is generally associated with observers' (Baker 1999: 641). Human interpreters intervene into communicative networks that include the exchange of signs within the world of geology as well as biology, amongst the non-living as well as the living.

As further evidence of this kind of geosemiotics, the sociologist Bronislaw Szerszynski draws on the nineteenth-century publication by David Thomas Ansted (1814–1880) in support of the semiotic functioning of nature, and its implications (Szerszynski 2012). Ansted's book was called *The Great Stone Book of Nature* (Ansted 1863). Ansted invoked metaphors of communication (the transfer of signs) to account for geological processes. Pressures, flows, tremors, earthquakes and geothermal eruptions send forces from one part of the Earth's crust to another, and across vast distances. Fluids circulate through the system. Near the surface of the Earth, water 'circulates through the earth, as it passes from the sea to the sky, and as it returns in refreshing showers from the sky to the earth, and so back again to the ocean' (Ansted 1863: 46). Ansted thought that this circulation served to communicate, providing 'the connecting link between the power and the conveyer of power' (Ansted 1863: 46).

Figure 20 Evidence of geological sign processes, Rangárþing ytra, Suðurland, Iceland.
Source: Author.

Szerszynski recruits Ansted's *The Great Stone Book of Nature*, alluding to the page-like character of layers of geological sedimentation and the identification of signs such as deposits, folds, fault lines and fossils. The Earth's geology is available for the geologist, to be read as if chapters and sections in a book. Geology tells a story, with key moments, of calm and cataclysm, and with several interweaving stories. Peirce's pansemiotics extends from the living to the non-living, or at least the *other-living*.

The posthuman and speculative realism

In these respects, there is much in Peirce and his followers that equates to ideas within posthumanism, theories that the universe can be understood beyond the constraints imposed by human language and reason. Contrary to Humanism, posthumanism denies that humans, their tools, technologies, concepts and achievements should be at the centre of our understanding of the universe. Philosophers such as Quentin Meillassoux (2009) and Graham Harman (2011) argue that the universe is made up of objects beyond our thinking about them, in 'the great outdoors' (Meillassoux 2009: 7) independently of human perception, interpretation and purpose. Unlike either Positivism or Phenomenology, their philosophy traverses some difficult territory in order to provide a contemporary assault on anthropocentrism (Herbrechter 2013), and provide an intellectual context for design in the age of the Anthropocene.

For Harman there are sensual objects that we perceive (such as the keyboard I'm typing on, water bottle and wallet) and real objects (the same, but frequently out of my conscious awareness). Then there are the qualities of these objects: some are seen and available to my awareness – sticky, cool, empty (sensual qualities); most others are hidden from view. He advances the proposition that 'Wakeful humans confront strawberries and commando raids, a sleeper confronts the bed, and a pebble confronts the asphalt that it strikes as opposed to all the accidental details of the asphalt' (Harman 2011: 103). He has other terms to describe object–quality relationships such as 'fusion', 'allure', and 'causation'. Harman's human-sounding relationships between things are not intended to project 'human properties onto the non-human world' (Harman 2011: 46). For Harman, the crude comprehensions exercised between 'minerals and dirt are no less relations than are the sophisticated mental activity of humans' (Harman 2011: 46). Human mental activity is but a subset of something that is going on between objects in the world already: 'Instead of placing souls into sand and stones, we find something sandy and stony in the human soul' (Harman 2011: 46). This observation echoes William Blake's (1757–1827) poem that begins 'To see the World in a Grain of Sand and a Heaven in a Wild Flower', a holistic sentiment that has inspired many artists and designers, from John Ruskin (1819–1900) to Charles and Ray Eames (Eames and Eames 1977).

It is helpful to bring the insights of thinkers such as Quentin Meillassoux (2009) into line with the thinking of Peirce – or at least, there is an opportunity to compare and contrast Peirce's pragmatic realism with some thinking now about reality (100 years later). Meillassoux's contention is that the so-called linguistic turn in philosophy cannot keep up with advances in science – the explosion of knowledge and data, and the vastness of time and space with which it deals. Meillassoux is opposed to the view that everything known and knowable about the universe is mediated and constructed by human intellect, and in language. Along with others of the posthumanist and speculative realist schools, Meillassoux wants to allow the possibility of thinking and talking about a reality that does not depend on us humans. I think the challenge is to develop such a philosophy without resorting to old-fashioned naïve realism. Peircean pragmatism provides this path and ascribes to material tangible nature agency in the semiotic sphere, to which we humans contribute in ways significant to us. Peirce's explanations of the importance of signs and the communicative structures within and between all things, provides a simple entry point to such posthuman, non-anthropocentric notions. I think that Peirce's pansemiotics provides what posthumanists (like Harman and Meillassoux) want – a means of according agency, autonomy and meaning to objects like rocks and stones outside of what humans say about them. For the semiotician, the world is already caught up in sets of communicative relationships, in a field of signs, into which we human agents participate as long as we are around.

Peirce's explanations of the importance of signs and the communicative structures within and between all things, provides a simple entry point to such posthuman, non-anthropocentric notions.

CHAPTER 7

Pragmatism

To summarise, C.S. Peirce exerts his primary influence on architecture through his theory of signs. Signs run deep in the human psyche, our creations, the world of artifice and of nature. I think that the rival semiotic position of the Structuralists and their successors has held sway in mainstream architectural scholarship, displacing potential engagement with Peirce's semiotics. But unlike Structuralism's emphasis on human language as the mediator and creator of our world, Peirce's semiotics emphasises practical and embodied engagement. His classification of signs supports this practical orientation, particularly as it emphasises the character of the index, in what I ventured to portray in Chapter 4 as an 'indexical architecture'.

As we have seen, indexicality pertains to signs that emerge from their objects, signs that in turn relate to evidence and fact. Peirce's theory of abductive inference has currency in logic and similar instrumental domains of programming, machine learning, probability and statistics, that have received renewed attention from the digital humanities (Fish 2012). In Chapter 5, I suggested that abduction relates strongly to concepts of interpretation, that is, hermeneutics, as expounded in Phenomenology. The concept of abduction provides a bridge between instrumental design methods, computational design and artificial intelligence in architecture on the one hand, and Phenomenology on the other.

Peirce founded the school of thought known as Pragmatism. Pragmatism provides a main point of contact between Peirce and other twentieth-century thinkers. Postmodern cultural theorists were alerted to the significant links between American Pragmatism, neo-Marxist Critical Theory and Phenomenology through the writing of the philosopher Richard Rorty (1931–2007), which foregrounded Pragmatic scholars such as Peirce, William James and John

Dewey (Rorty 1980; Coyne 1995). Several diverse schools of thinking nod in the direction of Pragmatism. After all, Karl Marx advocated practical action to bring about social change, and asserted, 'All social life is essentially practical' (Marx 1977: 157). Phenomenology is also a pragmatic philosophy. It emphasises bodily engagement as opposed to idealised and abstract philosophical reflection. In *Being and Time*, one of Heidegger's earliest illustrations of being-in-the-world drew on the practical engagement of a carpenter with tools, and the implications of mishaps or breakdowns in the use of equipment (Heidegger 1962: 99). Pragmatism affirms embodiment and the engagement of the senses in human experience. It also asserts the formative power of technology in human affairs. The pragmatic attitude clearly resonates with the material, craft and embodied orientation of much architectural practice. Recall Broadbent's characterisation in Chapter 2 of 'pragmatic design' as emerging over time from circumstances, as evident in vernacular architecture.

Pragmatism provides a main point of contact between Peirce and other twentieth-century thinkers.

Influential in design theory and architecture, philosopher and urban planner Donald Schön (1930–1997) introduced the concept of *reflection in action*, which emphasised learning by doing, an overtly practical orientation (Schön 1983). Schön referenced both Peirce and John Dewey in his writing (Schön 1963). Then there is the recent move towards practice-led research in architecture and other professions (Smith and Dean 2009; Lucas 2016), the creative turn by which researchers and their supporters recognise that innovation, discovery and understanding come about through making as well as observing.

It is important to distinguish Peirce's pragmatic orientation from *utilitarianism*. In less imaginative hands, pragmatism reduces to decision-making intended to deliver the greatest good for the greatest number (Ryan 1987). Amongst the problems with utilitarianism, the numbers for whom the good is to apply are generally decided in a way that favours those in power. Disreputable organisations, sales personnel, advertisers, and politicians might seek actions that work successfully only for themselves and those in their orbit. Philosophical Pragmatism offers various antidotes to such opportunism, not least Peirce required that pragmatism operates in the social sphere, an orientation that he at one point described loosely as 'critical common-sensism' (Peirce 1998k: 420).

Pragmatism and positivism

Peirce's followers commonly set his Pragmatism in opposition to the philosophical movement known as *Logical Positivism*. Peirce himself defined Pragmatism in opposition to the analytical and theoretical orientation of Cartesian rationalism, which promoted the idea that we human beings are independent thinking subjects separate from the world of objects, and able to reason independently of the material circumstances we find ourselves in. For the rationalist, logic, number and symbol manipulation served as models of reasoning. The Logical Positivists of the 1920s also asserted the value of logic, and exerted considerable influence on architecture, both direct and indirect (Galison 1990). The direct influence came through aspects of functionalism and modernism, in building science and architectural engineering, and since the advent of computing in computer-aided design studies. The *indirect* influence came through the formation of the institutions and regulatory frameworks in which architecture is taught and practised. The influence of Logical Positivism was evident in early management studies, economic rationalism, top-down planning, goal setting, performance measures, and bureaucratisation. By some readings, Logical Positivism persists in the way institutions and organisations are monitored and regulated. The scientific management theories of Frederick Taylor (1856–1915) are linked historically to Logical Positivism. When people confront local authorities, funding councils and universities as overly managerial and bureaucratic, driven by performance indicators, customer satisfaction indexes, ledgers, business models and profit, they are often complaining against a legacy that has its grounding in Logical Positivism. The early work of the management theorist Herbert Simon also follows an avowed positivist trajectory, given clear expression in his advocacy of a 'science of design' (Simon 1969). Schön offered explicit challenge to Simon's advocacy of such a science.

Logical Positivism also provided a foil against which other movements have defined themselves. It is the proverbial straw man against which Pragmatists, Phenomenologists and Poststructuralists defined their cause and their approach to life and architecture. Logical positivism was one of the three dominant 'styles' of philosophy evident in the twentieth century according to philosopher of technology Don Ihde (1993). It developed in the 1920s and was sometimes identified as the Vienna Circle, with the logician Rudolph Carnap (1891–1970) amongst its leaders. Ihde's other two styles of philosophy are Phenomenology and Pragmatism. All three incorporate critiques of Cartesian rationalism, but, from the point of view of Pragmatism, Logical Positivism with its emphasis on logic and verification retains the strongest allegiance to the tenets of Descartes.

Peirce was hardly known to the logicians of the Vienna Circle and their successors. His ideas came late to their attention, but they saw his insights as a precursor to their own. One of the positivist successors was A.J. Ayer (1910–1989) who wrote a sympathetic but critical study of Peirce and Pragmatism (Ayer 1968).

Peirce's counter to rationalism is the *maxim of pragmatism*. Peirce introduced this rule as follows: 'Consider what effects that might conceivably have practical bearings we conceive the object of our conception to have: then, our conception of those effects is the whole of our conception of the object' (Peirce 1998c: 135).

This difficult passage requires some parsing. Peirce here puts the focus on 'practical bearings'. Any concept, such as justice, god, nature, technology, semiotics, architecture, a tree or a table, has no other scope or meaning than the practical difference it makes to hold to that concept. We could perhaps simplify the statement without losing too much: a concept has no other scope or meaning than the practical difference it makes to use that concept.

How does this practical orientation bear on signs and their classifications? It makes a practical difference whether the drawing (iconic sign) I have just created is of a house or a chair, or that we name such objects (via symbolic signs) as 'house' or 'chair'. There is a practical use context of our semiotic practices, in art as in everyday dealings. In case we are tempted to conflate the practical with the actual or real, Peirce asserted 'pragmatism is the doctrine that every conception is a conception of conceivable practical effects' (Peirce 1998c: 235). The processes by which we translate one set of symbols to another, as in deduction and induction, are also pragmatically defined, even in the case of imaginary logical propositions and rules. However, Peirce's pragmatic orientation is most evident in his concepts of *abduction*. Peirce argued, 'the maxim of pragmatism, if true, fully *covers* the entire logic of abduction' (Peirce 1998i: 235).

There is a practical use context of our semiotic practices, in art as in everyday dealings.

Peirce's doctrine of 'practical bearings' also comes through cogently in the case of the indexical sign. That an indexical sign constitutes evidence of its object via abduction fits the pragmatic orientation. The way detectives and diagnosticians gather, sift and process evidence (indexical signs) to identify the object of their investigations influences what they regard as relevant or irrelevant. Design as abduction also brings this pragmatic orientation to the fore.

That an indexical sign constitutes evidence of its object via abduction fits the pragmatic orientation.

As I have asserted elsewhere, for an architect the test of any philosophy is what difference it makes to the way architecture is practised, talked about, evaluated and taught (Coyne 2011: 1). In so far as we accept that orientation to philosophers and other thinkers, then we are aligned with Peirce's maxim of pragmatism.

for an architect the test of any philosophy is what difference it makes to the way architecture is practised, talked about, evaluated and taught

Verification

Pragmatism has its maxim. Logical Positivism rests similarly on a principle: the verification principle. This principle is of interest in so far as it has parallels to Peirce's pragmatism. According to Ayer, building on Carnap's logic, a statement can be emotionally significant, but if it does not meet the criterion of verifiability then it is 'not literally significant' (Ayer 1990: 16), that is, really significant. In *Language, Truth and Logic*, Ayer asserted,

> **The criterion which we use to test the genuineness of apparent statements of fact is the criterion of verifiability. We say that a sentence is factually significant to any given person, if, and only if, he knows how to verify the proposition which it purports to express – that is, if he knows what observations would lead him, under certain conditions, to accept the proposition as being true, or reject it as being false.**
>
> (1990: 16)

The verification principle, was formulated to dispose of certain difficult and abstruse philosophical questions as 'meaningless'. These Logical Positivists had in their sights philosophers such as Heidegger and others they thought promoted 'metaphysics', assertions about the fundamentals of existence that are after all impossible to verify. If you cannot think of a way to empirically test whether or not a proposition is true (e.g. by inspection, measurement, calculation or logic) then the proposition is meaningless whatever its value as a piece of provocative speculation or imaginative storytelling. The principle thereby would diminish the importance of architectural narratives about the primitive hut, origin myths, triadic thought and geosemiotics, and may even characterise them as meaningless.

Though Pierce's philosophy predated the Logical Positivists (the Vienna Circle) and the verification principle, his philosophy came late to their attention. Peirce scholar Albert Atkin provides a helpful summary of the similarities and differences between the verification principle and the maxim of pragmatism (Atkin 2016). There are indeed similarities. Many of a logical school of thought see Peirce's maxim as a progenitor to the verification principle, even though they were not necessarily aware of the maxim or its source. Peirce and the Logical Positivists both equate meaning with verification, observation and experience in some measure. Both respect the evidence of the senses to arbitrate in what is true, as opposed to a Cartesian styled abstract reasoning. Both draw on science, its methods, importance, findings and sense of progress as a model of reason, and both favour examples from science rather than ethics, aesthetics or other philosophical discourses. Both are strict in how they define what is appropriate for philosophical discussion according to their principles.

On the latter it is worth noting Ayer's declaration of the exclusive nature of his own position. He sought to clarify the logical relationships within science and philosophy: 'Consequently I maintain that there is nothing in the nature of philosophy to warrant the existence of conflicting philosophical "schools" ' (Ayer 1990: 10). So, he would resolve all disputes through logic.

By most accounts, even from its former adherents, Logical Positivism and the verification principle have fallen into disrepute, due to internal contradiction – the impossibility of verifying the verification principle by its own criterion, and its impracticality as a guiding principle for distinguishing truth, falsity, lies, meaning and relevance (Wittgenstein 1953). Though they had their day amongst architectural technologists, Simon, Carnap and Ayer have less intellectual influence on the content of architectural education than opponents from the schools of Pragmatism and Phenomenology. The rise of big data analytics and advanced computation may bring about a revival of Logical Positivism, though I hope I have shown that Peirce's pragmatism has more to offer the world of computation than Logical Positivism, a view affirmed by researchers in human–computer interaction design (McCarthy and Wright 2004). Whether or not through avowed allegiance, it is fair to say that Peirce's philosophy of Pragmatism currently has greater support in architectural discourse than Logical Positivism and has the added advantage of shedding light on processes of logic and computation.

Peirce's philosophy of Pragmatism currently has greater support in architectural discourse than Logical Positivism

The power of practice

Some of Peirce's ideas find their way into architecture and the arts via diverse channels and thinkers variously aligned with Pragmatism. Philosopher and feminist writer Julia Kristeva (1941–) championed a revised understanding of semiotics in the 1960s and is a major figure in the history of semiotics (Kristeva 1986). She has mentioned Peirce favourably in a few places, though her philosophy emerged mainly from the Structuralism of Saussure. Roland Barthes was amongst her teachers, and she was at the vanguard of the Poststructuralist movement. The radical philosopher Gilles Deleuze invoked Peirce's concepts of Firstness, Secondness and Thirdness in his account of cinema and absurdist comedy (Deleuze 2013a; Vellodi 2014), even proffering the concept of 'zeroness' (Deleuze 2013b: 30). Deleuze is an undisputed thinker for architects (Ballantyne 2007).

The philosopher Jacques Derrida, who has exerted considerable influence in architecture, drew on Peirce. Both spent time at Johns Hopkins University, separated by about 90 years. Peirce developed the concept of 'infinite semiosis' whereby signs refer to other signs, which in turn refer to other signs ad infinitum, that is, the paradoxical notion that signs chain together without ever seeming to alight firmly on a definitive object (Peirce 1992g: 51–2; Atkin 2016: 136–40). Derrida wrote much about the way meaning resides in the traces left by a trail of interrelated signs, and the putative grounding of truth and meaning on an infinite chessboard or a configuration of inter-reflecting mirrors. Derrida adopted Peirce's concepts in arguing that the illusive object, the thing ultimately represented by the sign 'functions only to give rise to an *interpretant* that itself becomes a sign and so on to infinity' (Derrida 1976: 49).

Michel Foucault (1926–1984) is another thinker whose relevance to architecture is well established (Fontana-Giusti 2013) and whose thinking others bring into alignment with Peirce. Peirce scholar Andrew Garner brings Peirce up against Foucault on the subject of power (Garnar 2006). As a pragmatist, Peirce wrote about actions and habits. But Peirce and the pragmatists were less concerned about matters of overt political power, assuming that the ultimate political goal is to bring people together in the exercise of goodwill. Pragmatism is a benign philosophy, as if borne of a less hostile age and political circumstance. Like Peirce, Foucault also wrote about actions and habits, but added insights about how human, bodily practices embed power relationships: the way we confine, discipline and train our bodies for example, not least in the architectures we construct. Foucault added an edge to the pragmatists' emphasis on action. For Foucault, human relationships are at their core agonistic. Like many twentieth-century Continental writers, Foucault was influenced by Karl Marx (1818–1883) and Friedrich Nietzsche (1844–1900), not to mention a century and a geopolitical context beset by revolutions and World Wars. Foucault turned the semiotic project into a story of conflict as society transitioned abruptly from one semiotic condition to another.

Foucault deployed concepts of the sign in his grand sweep of history. In his seminal book *The Order of Things*, Foucault divided European history into several epochs in terms of how societies deal with signs (Foucault 1970). The pre-classical period was governed by resemblance. The Classical Period was characterised by ordering and classification. This included reference to an exterior world. The nineteenth to the twentieth century is characterised by a reflection on language. We do not just use language, nor are we in it, but can objectify and study language critically, including its history and evolution. European society now acts as if emancipated, freed from the constraints of language by virtue of the conceit that we can study language objectively. Foucault's ideas about language and semiotics in turn informed historian Hayden White's influential theories about history and historiography (White 1978).

Radicalising Peirce

Throughout this book I have emphasised Peirce as a pragmatist whose thinking alights on the materiality of the physical world, emphasising 'practical bearings'. I have argued that this approach has much in common with the phenomenology and hermeneutics of Heidegger and Gadamer. Architecture is a practical matter after all, and any discussion of thinkers for architects eventually comes down to the question of what difference that thinking makes to architecture. In this final section I wish to position Peirce as a radical thinker.

To do so it is necessary to begin with a position described by some theorists as philosophical *conservatism* (Hirsch 1987). Most people would adhere to a desire to conserve value systems, institutions, social norms, autonomy, identity, material culture, and buildings and environments of note. In its more negative connotations conservatism is also identified with preserving the status quo, existing power structures, and keeping minorities and those that do not conform in their place. In this light, a conservative view of architecture is one that might over-value the architectural canon, the prime examples of what makes good architecture, iconic buildings and architects, whilst excluding others. It may also want to conserve, revive and promote what it sees as core architectural values, authority structures and rules. Extreme conservatism is often associated with intransigence, a closed mindset and a nostalgia for what was good and right as defined by those in authority. A conservative semiotics of architecture and art wishes to preserve the artistic canon and settle on interpretations that are of long standing and 'correct'.

According to hermeneutical scholars, this conservative political leaning seems to go hand-in-hand with a conservative approach to meaning (Gallagher 1992), which in turn impinges on semiotics. It is as if there is a decided meaning (interpretant) to important signs. For the conservative interpreter, such meanings come from two sources. First, are the socially sanctioned meanings grounded in traditional interpretations. Second, are authorial intentions: what the author, creator, designer, inventor meant by the thing they have created. A conservative semiotics typically involves interrogating a work of architecture, the record and its context for the intentions of the designer or author in creating the work in the first place. The final arbiter in the matter of the work of architecture's interpretation is what the architect meant by the work, whether or not the architect could put that into words. In the case of a historical work this process involves comparing and sifting evidence to uncover these authorial intentions, and of course debating the evidence for them. Such a conservative view gains support from the idea of impartiality, that it is necessary and possible to approach any philosophical problem (or interpretative situation) with a clear mind, that is, without the prejudice born of the interpreter's predispositions, current context and social conditions. This conservative approach might also suggest that under the right conditions, some users, viewers, or readers, by virtue of their authority and expertise, have immediate access to the artwork (text, building, design), or access to an *essence* of the architecture, that is independent of the situation of the experience. Conservative hermeneutics lays emphasis on experts and expertise.

Such conservatism also pertains to Ayer's support of the principle of verification, that an assertion is meaningful to the extent that it can be empirically verified, as either true or false. Such a view is conservative in a cultural sense in that it rules out provisional propositions, provocations, ambiguity and speculation, and partitions humour, absurdity, storytelling, myth, popular culture and mixed modes of textual and non-textual research and philosophical reflection from 'serious' thinking.

Peirce's pragmatic semiosis runs counter to conservatism and its variants. I have already referred to his statement about the contingency of the task of classifying signs. Though he started with logic, he broke it down to the contingent processes of abduction. In his essay 'The Fixation of Belief', Peirce accommodated cognitive characteristics such as tenacity, holding on to belief in spite of contrary evidence, of following the opinions of leaders, of following common sense and taste, and of course adopting findings from science (Peirce 1992c). In his account of Peirce's essays, Albert Atkin has noted that Peirce the pragmatist sidestepped issues of truth and reality in favour of the practical process of conducting an inquiry (Atkin 2016). For Peirce the pragmatist, inquiry proceeds from doubt to belief. At least by my reading, pragmatism puts the focus on process, and what difference it makes to believe (or doubt) one proposition or argument over another.

The main objections to semiotic and political conservatism come from critical theorists, such as those in the Frankfurt School of Continental philosophy and their contemporary advocates. A *critical* position is suspicious of all reasoning that already has an outcome in mind, that claims certainty, and constructs grand narratives of progress and purpose (Lyotard 1986). Early proponents of a critical position held discursive logic in contempt, as did Herbert Marcuse: 'the logic of thought remains the logic of domination' (Marcuse 1991: 138). In Chapter 2, I outlined how Structuralism supports this kind of critical, political discourse.

A further category of thinking and practice has often been characterised as *radical*. This is a style of thinking that is disruptive. It seeks out the elements in any discourse that disturb established ways of thinking. By most accounts, Poststructuralism and Derrida's thinking fall within this category, as does the thinking of Deleuze and many others. The radical posture brings to mind Bernard Tschumi's observation that 'the ultimate pleasure of architecture lies in the most forbidden parts of the architectural act; where limits are perverted, and prohibitions are transgressed. The starting point of architecture is distortion' (Tschumi 1994: 91; Armitage 2015).

These four intellectual categories of conservative, pragmatic, critical and radical provide a useful framework for characterising twentieth- and twenty-first-century thinking. They provide a crude but practically useful set of distinctions. The classification derives from hermeneutical scholarship and was ably presented in the context of educational philosophy by philosopher Shaun Gallagher (Gallagher 1992). The pragmatist (or moderate hermeneut) recognises the contingency of all interpretations. On the other hand, a conservative interpreter seeks authoritative and original intentions and meanings. For the critical hermeneut the task is to probe beneath the surface for evidence of domination and unequal and exploitative power relations. Finally, the *radical* seeks to subvert categories, or desires to assert new categories, and to challenge certainties, a journey familiar to architectural theorists.

the *radical* seeks to subvert categories, or desires to assert new categories, and to challenge certainties, a journey familiar to architectural theorists.

As for any thinker, there are elements of the pragmatic, conservative, critical and radical in each of us. Peirce was a radical thinker as well as a pragmatist, and others have adopted his thinking in a radical frame. Peirce's concept of the indexical sign can be so appropriated and shows that his work is up to date with some of the thinking about the posthuman, and concerns about environment, the Anthropocene, and technical matters pertaining to big data, surveillance and innovation. I have attempted to highlight some of these radical aspects of Peirce's thinking throughout this book. I hope I have demonstrated that the vast range of Peirce's oeuvre is worthy of detailed study within architecture.

Glossary

Abduction: A kind of reasoning that works backwards from a logical conclusion to the conditions that would make that conclusion true. Abduction features prominently in Peirce's characterisation of human reasoning from evidence. It also provides insights into design processes.

Argument: A rule, or collection of rules, of inference that gets passed between interlocutors in a spirited conversation: for example, what is your argument? This is one of Peirce's nine key terms that helps define a class of signs.

Communication: the transfer or sharing of signs.

Deconstruction: See Poststructuralism.

Delome: Peirce's alternative term for an argument.

Design Methods Movement: An intellectual movement in design education, research and practice beginning after WWII that sought to make the design process more scientific, by drawing on systems theory that was thought to underpin all disciplines. By some accounts it progressed through first-generation methods to less formal second-generation methods before its eventual dissipation in the 1980s.

Dicent: That characteristic of a sign that is complete and self-contained, as when a street vendor draws attention to a product by calling out its name: 'Big Issue!'.

Firstness, Secondness and Thirdness: Peirce's ontological categories progressing from immediate, qualitative experience (Firstness), to expressions about those experiences (Secondness) to complex discursive statements and arguments (Thirdness). It was important to Peirce that Thirdness depends on Secondness, which in turn depends on Firstness. He used these categories and their dependencies as a way of structuring his classifications of signs.

Hermeneutics: The study of interpretation mainly as developed and championed by Hans-Georg Gadamer, drawing on Martin Heidegger, and the Phenomenological tradition.

Icon: That characteristic of a sign that operates through resemblance. So, a drawing of a building operates as a sign if it resembles it (i.e. if it is a 'good likeness').

Index: That characteristic of a sign that operates by virtue of emerging from its object. Smoke is a sign of fire in that the smoke emanates from, or is caused by, the fire – directly and inevitably. A photograph is also an index of its object as there is an optical-mechanical process linking the sign (photograph) to its object (the subject in the photograph). (Note that the photograph is also an iconic sign.) Pointing at something is also an indexical sign in that it indicates its object directly and inevitably.

Information: Peirce referred to 'information' as what a sign conveys. I take 'information' to be subsumed within the concept of the *interpretant*, though Peirce does not make this explicit, and it is fair to say that he used the term 'information' informally.

Interpretant: The effect of a sign on the person, agent or entity that receives the sign. This includes the meaning, interpretation or action that may follow from the sign. Peirce also referred to the interpretant as an 'idea in the mind that the sign excites' (Peirce 1998h: 13).

Langue: This is Saussure's term for the deep structure of a language evident in underlying principles or rules that pervade all human languages.

Legisign: A characteristic of a sign that is determined by convention. Words and symbols are typically legisigns

	in that you have to learn the conventions or rules of their use. A diagram of a class of buildings, or other generalised drawing, would also be a legisign.
Object:	What a sign references, points to, indexes, resembles or symbolises. It can be a physical, imaginary or virtual object, an idea, a concept or another sign.
OED:	Oxford English Dictionary.
Parole:	This is Saussure's term for the surface structure of a language evident in accent, dialect and idiom.
Poststructuralism:	The school of thought that radicalises Saussure's Structuralism, following Jacques Derrida and others.
Qualisign:	That qualitative aspect of a sign which operates irrespective of the medium it appears in. Such a quality can relate to features such as colour, texture, temperature, weight, beauty and ugliness, as well as their qualification: too heavy, too red, not red enough, etc.
Referent:	The thing to which a sign refers. Peirce used the term 'object' rather than 'referent'. Saussure used the term 'signified'.
Rheme:	A rheme is a part of a statement in language, a partial proposition that needs the rest of the proposition to make sense. For Peirce, pronouns are rhemes. They are incomplete without some other sign of the thing (object) to which they refer. There is a basic, primitive, qualitative aspect to the incompleteness of the rheme, which for Peirce places it in the category of Firstness.
Semeiotics, semiotics, semiology:	The study and use of signs.
Sign:	According to the OED, a sign is 'An action, mark, notice, etc., conveying information or instructions, and related senses'.
Sign situation:	This is the general term used by followers of Saussure for the relationship between the signifier and signified in any particular case.

Sign-vehicle: The aspect of a sign that directs attention to its object. In the case of a weathervane as a sign of the wind direction, it is the orientation of the vane that acts as the sign-vehicle, not the colour or other properties of the weathervane.

Signified: Saussure's term for the object, thing, concept or idea being referred to in a sign situation.

Signifier: Saussure's term for the entity that does the signifying in a sign situation, usually this is a word, picture or sound. It roughly relates to a sign or sign-vehicle in Peirce's broader nomenclature in which human language is not so central to the idea of the sign.

Sinsign: That aspect of a sign that operates as a singular sign, a one-off, as opposed to a sign that refers to a class of objects. A floor plan of a particular building is a sinsign. It excludes a diagram of a building type. Such a general diagram would be a legisign.

Structuralism: A school of thought that adopts Saussure's theories about the binary structure of the sign.

Symbol: That aspect of a sign established through social convention, as in the case of mathematical symbols, abstract tokens, or spoken or written language. Symbols are always legisigns, but Peirce indicates that they can be further qualified as rhemes, dicents or arguments.

Further reading

For an explanation of his sign classification system see Peirce, C.S., 'Nomenclature and Divisions of Triadic Relations, As Far As They Are Determined', in N. Houser (ed.), *The Essential Peirce, Selected Philosophical Writings Volume 2 (1893–1913)*, Bloomington, IN: Indiana University Press, 1998, 289–99.

For his examination of abduction see Peirce, C.S., 'Pragmatism as the Logic of Abduction', in N. Houser (ed.), *The Essential Peirce, Selected Philosophical Writings Volume 2 (1893–1913)*, Bloomington, IN: Indiana University Press, 1992, 226–41.

Broadbent introduces Peirce to an architectural audience in Broadbent, G., 'Building Design as an Iconic Sign System', in G. Broadbent, R. Bunt and C. Jencks (eds), *Signs, Symbols, and Architecture*, Chichester: John Wiley and Sons, 1980, 311–31.

For the major account of Peirce's theory of abduction applied to design in architecture see March, L., 'Introduction: The Logic of Design and the Question of Value', in L. March (ed.), *The Architecture of Form*, London: Cambridge University Press, 1976, 1–40.

Two major publications examining Peirce's theories in the context of architecture are by Umbert Eco and Donald Preziosi. See Eco, U., 'Function and Sign: The Semiotics of Architecture', in G. Broadbent, R. Bunt and C. Jencks (eds), *Signs, Symbols, and Architecture*, Chichester: John Wiley and Sons, 1980, 11–69; and Preziosi, D., *Architecture, Language and Meaning: Origins of the Built World and Its Semiotic Organization*, The Hague, The Netherlands: Mouton, 1979.

For a recent account of Peirce's theories see Atkin, A., *Peirce*, Abingdon, Oxon: Routledge, 2016.

For a full account of semiotics, including Peirce's theories, across many disciplines see Nöth, W., *Handbook of Semiotics*, Bloomington IN: Indiana University Press, 1990. *The Stanford Encyclopedia of Philosophy* also provides valuable, authoritative accounts of Peirce's philosophy. See Burch, R., 'Charles Sanders Peirce'. *The Stanford Encyclopedia of Philosophy* (Fall 2017 Edition). Available at: https://plato.stanford.edu/archives/fall2017/entries/peirce/ (accessed 17 November 2017).

For my own account of Peirce's relevance to the natural environment and biosemiotics, see Coyne, R., *Network Nature: The Place of Nature in the Digital Age*, London: Bloomsbury Academic, 2018. I also reference Peirce's theories in blog postings. See Coyne, R., 'Peirce Decoded'. *Reflections on Technology, Media and Culture*, 30 December, 2017. Available at: https://richardcoyne.com/2017/12/30/peirce-decoded/ (accessed 28 April 2018).

References

Alexander, C. (1964) *Notes on the Synthesis of Form*, Cambridge, MA: Harvard University Press.

Alexander, C., S. Ishikawa and M. Silverstein. (1977) *A Pattern Language: Towns, Buildings, Construction*, New York: Oxford University Press.

Anderson, D. (1984) 'Peirce on Metaphor', *Transactions of the Charles S. Peirce Society*, 20 (4): 453–68.

Ansted, D.T. (1863) *The Great Stone Book of Nature*, London: Macmillan & Co.

Armitage, J. (2015) *Virilio for Architects*, Abingdon, Oxon: Routledge.

Armstrong, R. (2015) *Vibrant Architecture: Matter as a Codesigner of Living Structures*, Warsaw: Gruyter Open.

Atkin, A. (2016) *Peirce*, Abingdon, Oxon: Routledge.

Atzori, L., A. Iera and G. Morabito. (2010) 'The Internet of Things: A Survey', *Computer Networks*, 54: 2787–805.

Awbrey, J. (2008) 'Logical Graphs: 1', *Inquiry Into Inquiry*, 29 July. Available at: https://inquiryintoinquiry.com/2008/07/29/logical-graphs-1/ (accessed 4 February 2018).

Ayer, A.J. (1968) *The Origins of Pragmatism: Studies in the Philosophy of Charles Sanders Peirce and William James*, London: Macmillan.

Ayer, A.J. (1990) *Language, Truth and Logic*, London: Penguin.

Baker, V.R. (1999) 'Geosemiosis', *Bulletin of the Geological Society of America*, 111 (5): 633–45.

Ballantyne, A. (2007) *Deleuze and Guattari for Architects*, London: Routledge.

Barr, A., E.A. Feigenbaum and P.R. Cohen. (1981) *The Handbook of Artificial Intelligence*, Stanford, CA: HeurisTech Press.

Barthes, R. (1973) *Mythologies*, trans. A. Lavers, London: Paladin.

Beesley, P., S. Hirosue, J. Ruxton, M. Trankle and C. Turner. (2006) *Responsive Architectures: Subtle Technologies*, Toronto, Ontario: Riverside Architectural Press.

Bordeleau, A. (2008) 'An Indexical Approach to Architecture', *Footprint: Delft Architectural Theory Journal*, (3): 79–96.

Botar, O. (2016) 'The Biocentric Bauhaus', in C.N. Terranova and M. Tromble (eds), *The Routledge Companion to Biology in Art and Architecture*, London: Routledge, 17–51.

Broadbent, G. (1969) 'Meaning into Architecture', in C. Jencks and G. Baird (eds), *Meaning in Architecture*, London: Barrie & Rockliff, 50–75.

Broadbent, G. (1973) *Design in Architecture: Architecture and the Human Sciences*, New York: John Wiley and Sons.

Broadbent, G. (1980) 'Building Design as an Iconic Sign System', in G. Broadbent, R. Bunt and C. Jencks (eds), *Signs, Symbols, and Architecture*, Chichester: John Wiley and Sons, 311–31.

Broadbent, G. and J. Glusberg (eds). (1991) *Deconstruction: A Student Guide*, London: Academy Editions.

Broadbent, G., R. Bunt and C. Jencks. (1980) *Signs, Symbols, and Architecture*, Chichester: John Wiley and Sons.

Burch, R. (2017) 'Charles Sanders Peirce', *The Stanford Encyclopedia of Philosophy (Fall 2017 Edition)*. Available at: https://plato.stanford.edu/archives/fall2017/entries/peirce/ (accessed 17 November 2017).

Chalmers, A.F. (1999) *What Is This Thing Called Science?* Indianapolis, IN: Hackett Publishing Co.

Clocksin, W.F. and C.S. Mellish. (1981) *Programming in Prolog*, Berlin: Springer-Verlag.

Coyne, R. (1988) *Logic Models of Design*, London: Pitman.

Coyne, R. (1995) *Designing Information Technology in the Postmodern Age: From Method to Metaphor*, Cambridge, MA: MIT Press.

Coyne, R. (2010) *The Tuning of Place: Sociable Spaces and Pervasive Digital Media*, Cambridge, MA: MIT Press.

Coyne, R. (2011) *Derrida for Architects*, Abingdon: Routledge.

Coyne, R. (2017) 'Peirce Decoded', *Reflections on Technology, Media and Culture*, 30 December. Available at: https://richardcoyne.com/2017/12/30/peirce-decoded/ (accessed 28 April 2018).

Coyne, R. (2018) *Network Nature: The Place of Nature in the Digital Age*, London: Bloomsbury Academic.

Cramer, F. (2015) 'What Is "Post-Digital"?', in D.M. Berry and M. Dieter (eds), *Postdigital Aesthetics: Art, Computation and Design*, Basingstoke: Palgrave Macmillan, 12–26.

Daub-Schackat, R. (1996) 'Peirce and Hermeneutics', in V.M. Colapietro and T.M. Olshewsky (eds), *Peirce's Doctrine of Signs: Theory, Applications and Connections*, Berlin: Mouton de Gruyter, 381–91.

de Rivera, J. and C. Grinkis. (1986) 'Emotion as Social Relationships', *Motivation and Emotion*, 10 (4): 351–69.

De Souza, C.S. and S.D.J. Barbosa. (2006) 'A Semiotic Framing for End-User Development', in H. Lieberman, F. Paternò and V. Wulf (eds), *End User Development*, New York: Springer, 401–26.

Deleuze, G. (2013a) *Cinema I: The Movement-Image*, trans. H. Tomlinson and B. Habberjam, London: Bloomsbury Academic.

Deleuze, G. (2013b) *Cinema Ii: The Time-Image*, trans. H. Tomlinson and R. Galeta, London: Bloomsbury Academic.

Derrida, J. (1976) *Of Grammatology*, trans. G.C. Spivak, Baltimore, MD: Johns Hopkins University Press.

Derrida, J. (1986) 'Point De Folie: Maintenant L'architecture', in N. Leach (ed.), *Rethinking Architecture: A Reader in Cultural Theory*, London: Routledge, 305–17.

Dewey, J. (1958) *Experience and Nature*, New York: Dover.

Dorst, K. (2011) 'The Core of "Design Thinking" and Its Application', *Design Studies*, 32 (6): 521–32.

Durand, J.-N.-L. (2000) *Précis of the Lectures on Architecture*, trans. D. Britt, Los Angeles, CA: Getty Research Institute.

Eames, C. and R. Eames. (1977) *Powers of Ten* (Film), USA: IBM.

Eco, U. (1980) 'Function and Sign: The Semiotics of Architecture', in G. Broadbent, R. Bunt and C. Jencks (eds), *Signs, Symbols, and Architecture*, Chichester: John Wiley and Sons, 11–69.

Everaert-Desmedt, N. (2011) 'Peirce's Semiotics', *Signo*, Louis Hébert (dir.). Available at: www.signosemio.com/peirce/semiotics.asp (accessed 13 May 2018).

Fish, S. (2012) 'The Digital Humanities and the Transcending of Mortality', *Opinionator*, January. Available at: http://opinionator.blogs.nytimes.com/

2012/01/09/the-digital-humanities-and-the-transcending-of-mortality/?_php=true&_type=blogs&_r=0 (accessed 28 November 2018).

Fontana-Giusti, G. (2013) *Foucault for Architects*, Abingdon: Routledge.

Foucault, M. (1970) *The Order of Things: An Archaeology of the Human Sciences*, New York: Random House.

Freud, S. (1991) 'Infantile Sexuality', in A. Richards (ed.), *The Penguin Freud Library, Volume 7: On Sexuality*, Harmondsworth: Penguin, 88–126.

Gadamer, H.-G. (1975) *Truth and Method*, trans. J. Weinsheimer, New York: Seabury Press.

Galison, P. (1990) 'Aufbau/Bauhaus: Logical Positivism and Architectural Modernism', *Critical Inquiry*, 16 (4): 709–52.

Gallagher, S. (1992) *Hermeneutics and Education*, Albany, NY: SUNY Press.

Garnar, A. (2006) 'Power, Action, Signs: Between Peirce and Foucault', *Transactions of the Charles S. Peirce Society*, 42 (3): 347–66.

Glendinning, M. (2010) *Architecture's Evil Empire? The Triumph and Tragedy of Global Modernism*, London: Reaktion.

Gruber, P. (2011) *Biomimetics in Architecture*, Springer: Berlin.

Hale, J. (2016) *Merleau-Ponty for Architects*, London: Routledge.

Harman, G. (2011) *The Quadruple Object*, Winchester: Zero Books.

Hawkes, T. (2003) *Structuralism and Semiotics*, London: Routledge.

Heidegger, M. (1962) *Being and Time*, trans. J. Macquarrie and E. Robinson, London: SCM Press.

Heidegger, M. (1971) 'Building, Dwelling, Thinking', *Poetry, Language, Thought*, New York: Harper and Rowe, 143–61.

Heidegger, M. (1981) *Poetry, Language, Thought*, trans. A. Hofstadter, New York: Harper and Row.

Herbrechter, S. (2013) *Posthumanism: A Critical Analysis*, London: Bloomsbury Academic.

Hernández, F. (2010) *Bhabha for Architects*, London: Routledge.

Heyworth, R. (2014) 'Monte Alban: The Encrypted City', *Uncovered History*, 16 April. Available at: https://uncoveredhistory.com/mexico/monte-alban-the-encrypted-city/ (accessed 23 September 2017).

Hirsch, E.D. (1987) *Cultural Literacy: What Every American Needs to Know*, Boston, MA: Houghton Mifflin.

Houser, N. (1998) 'Introduction', in N. Houser (ed.), *The Essential Peirce, Selected Philosophical Writings, Volume 2 (1893–1913)*, Bloomington, IN: Indiana University Press, xvii–xxxviii.

Ihde, D. (1993) *Philosophy of Technology: An Introduction*, New York: Paragon.

Jencks, C. (1980) 'The Architectural Sign', in G. Broadbent, R. Bunt and C. Jencks (eds), *Signs, Symbols, and Architecture*, Chichester: John Wiley and Sons, 71–118.

Jencks, C. (2005) *Iconic Building*, New York: Rizzoli.

Jencks, C. and G. Baird (eds) (1969) *Meaning in Architecture*, London: Barrie & Rockliff.

Jencks, C. and K. Kropf (eds) (1997) *Theories and Manifestoes of Contemporary Architecture*, Chichester: Wiley-Academic.

Jones, J.C. (1970) *Design Methods: Seeds of Human Futures*, London: Wiley.

Khan, A. and P. Wu Wu. (2017) 'U-232 & Biobots', *The Entropy Project*. Available at: www.theentropyproject.com/biobots (accessed 13 June 2018).

Khan, A. (2018) '29.9511° N, 90.0715° W', *The Entropy Project*. Available at: www.theentropyproject.com/xenohowls (accessed 13 June 2018).

Kidder, P. (2013) *Gadamer for Architects*, Abingdon: Routledge.

Kitchin, R. (2014) 'The Real-Time City? Big Data and Smart Urbanism', *GeoJournal*, 79: 1–14.

Koskela, L., S. Paavola and E. Kroll. (2017) 'The Role of Abduction in Production of New Ideas in Design', in P.E. Vermaas and S. Vial (eds), *Advancements in the Philosophy of Design*, Cham, Switzerland: Springer, 153–83.

Krauss, R. (1977) 'Notes on the Index: Seventies Art in America', *October*, 3: 68–81.

Kristeva, J. (1986) 'Word, Dialogue and Novel', in T. Moi (ed.), *The Kristeva Reader*, New York: Columbia University Press, 34–61.

Kruse, F.E. (1986) 'Indexicality and the Abductive Link', *Transactions of the Charles S. Peirce Society*, 22 (4): 435–47.

Langrish, J.Z. (2016) *The Design Methods Movement: From Optimism to Darwinism (Conference Presentation)*, Brighton: Design Research Society.

Laugier, M.-A. (1977) *An Essay on Architecture*, trans. W. Herrmann and A. Herrmann, Los Angeles, CA: Hennessey and Ingalls.

Leja, M. (2000) 'Peirce, Visuality, and Art', *Representations*, 72: 97–122.

Lévi-Strauss, C. (1963) *Structural Anthropology 1*, trans. C. Jacobson and B.G. Schoepf, New York: Basic Books.

Locke, J. (1976) *An Essay Concerning Human Understanding*, London: Fontana.

Lucas, R. (2016) *Research Methods in Architecture*, London: Laurence King.

Lyotard, J.-F. (1986) *The Postmodern Condition: A Report on Knowledge*, Manchester: Manchester University Press.

March, L. (1976) 'Introduction: The Logic of Design and the Question of Value', in L. March (ed.), *The Architecture of Form*, London: Cambridge University Press, 1–40.

Marcuse, H. (1991) *One-Dimensional Man: Studies in the Ideology of Advanced Industrial Society*, London: Routledge.

Marinetti, F.T. (1909) 'The Founding and Manifesto of Futurism', *Le Figaro*, February 20.

Marx, K. (1977) 'Theses on Feuerbach', in D. McClellan (ed.), *Karl Marx: Selected Writings*, Oxford: Oxford University Press, 156–8.

McCarthy, J. and P. Wright. (2004) *Technology as Experience*, Cambridge, MA: MIT Press.

McEwen, I. (2003) *Vitruvius: Writing the Body of Architecture*, Cambridge, MA: MIT Press.

Meillassoux, Q. (2009) *After Finitude: An Essay on the Necessity of Contingency*, London: Continuum.

Nöth, W. (1990) *Handbook of Semiotics*, Bloomington, IN: Indiana University Press.

Ogden, C.K. and I.A. Richards. (1989) *The Meaning of Meaning: A Study of the Influence of Language Upon Thought and of the Science of Symbolism*, Orlando, FL: Harvest.

Ong, W.J. (1972) *Ramus: Method, and the Decay of Dialogue from the Art of Discourse to the Art of Reason*, New York: Octagon.

Peirce, C.S. (1965) *The Collected Papers of Charles Sanders Peirce Volumes 1–8*, Cambridge, MA: Harvard University Press.

Peirce, C.S. (1992a) *The Essential Peirce, Selected Philosophical Writings, Volume 1 (1867–1893)*, Bloomington, IN: Indiana University Press.

Peirce, C.S. (1992b) 'The Architecture of Theories', in N. Houser and C. Kloesel (eds), *The Essential Peirce, Selected Philosophical Writings Volume 1 (1867–1893)*, Bloomington, IN: Indiana University Press, 285–97.

Peirce, C.S. (1992c) 'The Fixation of Belief', in N. Houser and C. Kloesel (eds), *The Essential Peirce, Selected Philosophical Writings, Volume 1 (1867–1893)*, Bloomington, IN: Indiana University Press, 106–23.

Peirce, C.S. (1992d) 'On the Algebra of Logic: A Contribution to the Philosophy of Notation (1886)', in N. Houser and C. Kloesel (eds), *The Essential Peirce, Selected Philosophical Writings, Volume 1 (1867–1893)*, Bloomington, IN: Indiana University Press, 225–8.

Peirce, C.S. (1992e) 'A Guess at the Riddle', in N. Houser and C. Kloesel (eds), *The Essential Peirce, Selected Philosophical Writings, Volume 1 (1867–1893)*, Bloomington, IN: Indiana University Press, 245–79.

Peirce, C.S. (1992f) 'Questions Concerning Certain Faculties Claimed for Man', in N. Houser and C. Kloesel (eds), *The Essential Peirce, Selected Philosophical Writings, Volume 1 (1867–1893)*, Bloomington, IN: Indiana University Press, 11–27.

Peirce, C.S. (1992g) 'Some Consequences of Four Incapacities', in N. Houser and C. Kloesel (eds), *The Essential Peirce, Selected Philosophical Writings, Volume 1 (1867–1893)*, Bloomington, IN: Indiana University Press, 28–55.

Peirce, C.S. (1998a) *The Essential Peirce, Selected Philosophical Writings, Volume 2 (1893–1913)*, Bloomington, IN: Indiana University Press.

Peirce, C.S. (1998b) 'Immortality in the Light of Synechism', in N. Houser (ed.), *The Essential Peirce, Selected Philosophical Writings, Volume 2 (1893–1913)*, Bloomington, IN: Indiana University Press, 1–3.

Peirce, C.S. (1998c) 'The Maxim of Pragmatism', in N. Houser (ed.), *The Essential Peirce, Selected Philosophical Writings, Volume 2 (1893–1913)*, Bloomington, IN: Indiana University Press, 133–44.

Peirce, C.S. (1998d) 'What Is a Sign?', in N. Houser (ed.), *The Essential Peirce, Selected Philosophical Writings, Volume 2 (1893–1913)*, Bloomington, IN: Indiana University Press, 4–10.

Peirce, C.S. (1998e) 'Nomenclature and Divisions of Triadic Relations, as Far as They Are Determined', in N. Houser (ed.), *The Essential Peirce, Selected*

Philosophical Writings, Volume 2 (1893–1913), Bloomington, IN: Indiana University Press, 289–99.

Peirce, C.S. (1998f) 'Sundry Logical Conceptions', in N. Houser (ed.), *The Essential Peirce, Selected Philosophical Writings, Volume 2 (1893–1913)*, Bloomington, IN: Indiana University Press, 267–88.

Peirce, C.S. (1998g) 'Excerpts from Letters to Lady Welby', in N. Houser (ed.), *The Essential Peirce, Selected Philosophical Writings, Volume 2 (1893–1913)*, Bloomington, IN: Indiana University Press, 477–91.

Peirce, C.S. (1998h) 'Of Reasoning in General', in N. Houser (ed.), *The Essential Peirce, Selected Philosophical Writings, Volume 2 (1893–1913)*, Bloomington, IN: Indiana University Press, 11–26.

Peirce, C.S. (1998i) 'Pragmatism as the Logic of Abduction', in N. Houser (ed.), *The Essential Peirce, Selected Philosophical Writings, Volume 2 (1893–1913)*, Bloomington, IN: Indiana University Press, 226–41.

Peirce, C.S. (1998j) 'The Basis of Pragmaticism in the Normative Sciences', in N. Houser (ed.), *The Essential Peirce, Selected Philosophical Writings, Volume 2 (1893–1913)*, Bloomington, IN: Indiana University Press, 371–97.

Peirce, C.S. (1998k) 'Pragmaticism', in N. Houser (ed.), *The Essential Peirce, Selected Philosophical Writings, Volume 2 (1893–1913)*, Bloomington, IN: Indiana University Press, 398–433.

Peirce, C.S. (1998l) 'The Three Normative Sciences', in N. Houser (ed.), *The Essential Peirce, Selected Philosophical Writings, Volume 2 (1893–1913)*, Bloomington, IN: Indiana University Press, 196–207.

Peirce, C.S. (1998m) 'What Makes Reasoning Sound', in N. Houser (ed.), *The Essential Peirce, Selected Philosophical Writings, Volume 2 (1893–1913)*, Bloomington, IN: Indiana University Press, 242–57.

Perez-Gomez, A. (2016) *Attunement: Architectural Meaning after the Crisis of Modern Science*, Cambridge, MA: MIT Press.

Picon, A. (2015) *Smart Cities: A Spatialised Intelligence*, London: Wiley.

Plato. (1997) 'Cratylus', in J.M. Cooper (ed.), *Complete Works*, Indianapolis, IN: Hackett, 101–56.

Popov, V., M. Kosinski, D. Stillwell and B. Kielczewski. (2018) 'Apply Magic Source: Trait Prediction Engine'. *University of Cambridge Psychometrics Centre*. Available at: https://applymagicsauce.com/ (accessed 28 June 2018).

Preziosi, D. (1979) *Architecture, Language and Meaning: Origins of the Built World and Its Semiotic Organization*, The Hague, The Netherlands: Mouton.

Rawes, P. (2007) *Irigaray for Architects*, London: Routledge.

Ricoeur, P. (1977) *The Rule of Metaphor*, trans. R. Czerny, K. McLaughlin and J. Costello, London: Routledge and Kegan Paul.

Riemer, I. (1996) 'Hermeneutic Aspects in the Light of Peirce's Semiotics', in V.M. Colapietro and T.M. Olshewsky (eds), *Peirce's Doctrine of Signs: Theory, Applications and Connections*, Berlin: Mouton de Gruyter, 392–7.

Risselada, M. and D. van den Heuvel (eds). (2005) *Team 10: In Search of a Utopia of the Present 1953–81*, Rotterdam: NAi.

Romanini, V. (2009) 'The Periodic Table of Classes of Signs', *Minute Semeiotic*. Available at: www.minutesemeiotic.org/home.php?id=1 (accessed 2 December 2017).

Rorty, R. (1980) *Philosophy and the Mirror of Nature*, Oxford: Basil Blackwell.

Russolo, L. (2004) *The Art of Noise (Futurist Manifesto, 1913)*, trans. R. Filliou, New York: ubu classics.

Ryan, A. (ed.). (1987) *John Stuart Mill and Jeremy Bentham: Utilitarianism and Other Essays*, London: Penguin.

Saussure, F. de. (1983) *Course in General Linguistics*, trans. R. Harris, London: Duckworth.

Saussure, F. de. (1996) 'Linguistic Value', in P. Cobley (ed.), *The Communication Theory Reader*, London: Routledge, 99–114.

Schmidt, B. (2018) 'Adjectives'. *Directory of Mark Twain's Maxims, Quotations, and Various Opinions*. Available at: www.twainquotes.com/Adjectives.html (accessed 17 May 2018).

Schön, D. (1963) *Displacement of Concepts*, London: Tavistock.

Schön, D.A. (1983) *Reflective Practitioner: How Professionals Think in Action*, London: Temple Smith.

Sebeok, T.A. (1999) *Signs: An Introduction to Semiotics*, Toronto: University of Toronto Press.

Shank, G. and D.J. Cunningham. (1996) 'Modeling the Six Modes of Peircean Abduction for Educational Purposes', Indiana University. Available at: www.cs.indiana.edu/event/maics96/Proceedings/shank.html (accessed 2 February 2018).

Sharr, A. (2007) *Heidegger for Architects*, London: Routledge.

Shawcross, G. (2012) 'Visual Thinking', *Order, Rhythm and Pattern*, 12 December. Available at: https://grahamshawcross.com/2012/12/12/visual-thinking/ (accessed 18 June 2018).

Simon, H. (1969) *The Sciences of the Artificial*, Cambridge, MA: MIT Press.

Smith, H. and R.T. Dean. (2009) *Practice-Led Research, Research-Led Practice in the Creative Arts*, Edinburgh: Edinburgh University Press.

Snodgrass, A. and R. Coyne. (2006) *Interpretation in Architecture: Design as a Way of Thinking*, London: Routledge.

Spinks, C.W. (1991) *Peirce and Triadomania: A Walk in the Semiotic Wilderness*, Berlin: Walter de Gruyter.

Szerszynski, B. (2012) 'The End of the End of Nature: The Anthropocene and the Fate of the Human', *Oxford Literary Review*, 34 (2): 165–84.

Szerszynski, B. (2017) 'Gods of the Anthropocene: Geo-Spiritual Formations in the Earth's New Epoch', *Theory, Culture and Society*, 34 (2–3): 253–75.

Tanizaki, J. (1977) *In Praise of Shadows*, trans. T.J. Harper and E.G. Seidensticker, Stony Creek, CT: Leete's Island Books.

Tschumi, B. (1994) *Architecture and Disjunction*, Cambridge, MA: MIT Press.

Turner, B. (2010) 'V&A at Dundee Proposals Unveiled', *de zeen*, 28 September. Available at: www.dezeen.com/2010/09/28/va-at-dundee-proposals-unveiled/ (accessed 25 June 2018).

Veblen, T. (1998) *The Theory of the Leisure Class*, Amherst, NY: Promethius.

Vellodi, K. (2014) 'Diagrammatic Thought: Two Forms of Constructivism in C.S. Peirce and Gilles Deleuze', *Parrhesia*, (19): 79–95.

Vitruvius, P. (1960) *Vitruvius: The Ten Books on Architecture*, trans. M.H. Morgan, New York: Dover Publications.

Walther, E. (1974) *Allgemeine Zeichenlehre: Einführung in Die Grundlagen Der Semiotik [General Semiotic Theory: Introduction to the Basics of Semiotics]*, Stuttgart: Deutsche Verlags-Anstalt.

Weizman, E. (2017) *Forensic Architecture: Violence at the Threshold of Detectability*, Brooklyn, NY: Zone Books.

Weizman, E. (2018) 'Forensic Architecture'. Available at: www.forensic-architecture.org/ (accessed 26 May 2018).

Weizman, E., C. Varvia and R. Birkett. (2018) 'Counter Investigations: Forensic Architecture', The Institute of Contemporary Arts (ICA) London, 7 March – 13 May 2018. Available at: www.forensic-architecture.org/exhibition/counter-investigations/ (accessed 26 May 2018).

White, H. (1978) *Tropics of Discourse: Essays in Cultural Criticism*, Baltimore, MD: Johns Hopkins University Press.

Willis, K.S. and A. Aurigi. (2018) *Digital and Smart Cities*, Abingdon: Routledge.

Wittgenstein, L. (1953) *Philosophical Investigations*, trans. G.E.M. Anscombe, Oxford: Blackwell.

Wood, D. (2016) *A Visual Phenomenological Methodology: The Repositioning of Visual Communication Design as a Fresh Influence on Interaction Design (PhD Thesis)*, Edinburgh: The University of Edinburgh.

Zimmerman, C. (2012) 'Photography into Building in Post-War Architecture: The Smithsons and James Stirling', *Association of Art Historians*, 35 (2): 270–87.

Index

Note: Page numbers in **bold** refer to tables; those in *italic* to figures.

abduction 65–7, 73, 114; and architecture 70; automated 76; design 83–7; and evidence 82; and hermeneutics 80–1, 88–9; and pragmatism 105; and rheme 82; and the smart city 74–5
Alexander, C. 84, 91
analogical design 25–6
Ansted, D.T. 97–8
anthropocene 5, 98, 113
architecture: and abduction 70; and education 105, 107; forensic 76, 78–9; iconic 23–5, 110; indexical 2, 8, 58, 60, 77–9; and language 1, 11; and Peirce 1–5; responsive 78; and sign 27–8
argument 37, **41**, **42**, 45, **45**, 63, 114
argument symbolic legisign 37, **41**
artificial intelligence 101
Atkin, A. 5–6, 31, 46, 106, 111, 119
Ayer, A.J. 104, 106–7, 111

bang 51
Barthes, R. 17–19, 108
belief 67, 80, 111
big data 74, 107, 113
BIM (building information modelling) 63
binary structure 14–17, 52, 117

biomimesis 8, 25, 91
bricolage 17
Blake, W. 99
Broadbent, G. 2–3, 11–12, 23, 25–7, 118

Carnap, R. 104, 106–7
Cartesian rationalism 103–4, 107
cipher 57
code 25, 57, 78, 94; genetic 90
common sense 80, 111
communication 27, 95–7, 114
computer-aided design 63, 103
contrail 62–3
crime 67, 82–3; scene 83
critical common-sensism 103
critical theory 101, 112
cry 35–6, **40**, 44

data: analytics 74, 107; big 74, 107, 113
de Quincy, Quatremére 27
deconstruction 3, 26
deduction 64–5, 70–3, 75–6, 84, 87–9
Deleuze, G. 108
delome 37, **42**, **45**, 114
delomic indexical qualisign 48

Derrida, J. 18, 108, 112
Descartes, R. 104
design 8, 23, 25–7, 61, 67, 83–4; as abduction 83, 105, 114
design method 12, 26, 101
Design Methods Movement 26, 84, 114
detective 66, 75, 105
Dewey, J. 6, 102
diagnosis 82, 105
diagram 4, 32, **40**, 69, 87, 116
diagrammatic proof 67–9, 71
dicent 35, 117, **40**, **42**, **45**, 114
dicent iconic legisign 46, 48
dicent indexical legisign 35–6, **40**
dicent indexical sinsign 36, 39, **40**, 46, 50–1
dicent sinsign 50
dicent symbol 63, 71, 88
dicent symbolic legisign 37, **41**
digital footprint 76
Durand, J.-N.-L. 32, 40, 91

Eames, R. 99
Eco, U. 3, 12, 118
emotion 48, 106
evidence 66–7, 70–88, 105, 114
explosion 33, 51

Facebook 75–6
facts and signs 61–4
fire, sign of 33, **40**, 59, 61, 64–6, 115
firstness 41, 43–5, 114
firstness, secondness, thirdness 39, **45**, 46, 53–4, 108, 114

floor plan 32, 117
forensic architecture 76, 78–9
Foucault, M. 109
fourness 54
functionalism 77–8, 103

Gadamer, H.-G. 80, 87–9, 115
geometry 68
geosemiotics 96–7
gesture 36, **40**, 43
grammar 34, 36, 45, 50

habit 75–6, 80, 109
Harman, G. 54–5, 98–9
Heidegger, M. 43, 54, 102
hermeneutics 80, 87, 111, 115
Hertzberger, H. 19
hyperlink 35

icon 31–3, **40**, **42**, **45**; in architecture 23; definition 21–3, 25, 62, 115; and firstness 44; in nature 93
icon, index and symbol 12, 21–3, 26–7, 38, **42**
iconic architecture 23–5, 110
iconic legisign 32, 34, 69, 71
iconic qualisign 31
iconic sinsign 32
iconography 23–4
Ihde, D. 104
indefinite inference 80–2
index 2, 33–6, **40**, **42**, **45**, 59; book 35, 37; definition 9, 21, 61, 115; and evidence 64, 66–7, 105; and

facts 61–3; and nature 93–4; and secondness 44; and symbol 63–4
indexical architecture 2, 8, 58, 60, 77–9
indexicality 9, 59, 64, 80, 84, 101; shift to 59, 61
induction 65, 72–3, 82, 84
inference 8, 37, **41**, 67, 70; indefinite 80–2
infinite semiosis 108
information 31, 50, 96, 115
interaction design 10, 107
interpretant 7–8, 29–30, 38, **42**, **45**, 115
interpretation 30, 81, 101, 110–11, 115; and abduction 87–9

James, W. 6, 101
Jencks, C. 2, 11, 24, 58, 118

Kahn, L. 63
Kristeva, J. 108
Kuma, Kengo 60

language, 14, 95, 109; and architecture 1, 11; and difference 17; human 15, 91, 98, 101; and reality 14–15, 29; see also meaning; semiotics; structuralism
langue 17–18, 115
Laugier, Abé 27, 91
legisign 34–5, **40–2**, 50, 115
Lévi-Strauss, C. 16–17
LiDAR 79
Linguistics 11

Locke, J. 10–11, 14, 64
logic 1, 21, 37, 58, 70–3, 103; diagrams 69; limits to 80–1, 89; see also abduction; deduction; inference; logical positivism; syllogism
logical positivism 103–4, 106–7
Lyotard, J.-F. 112

machine learning 73, 76, 101
man is a sign 89, 95
map 32, 40, 96
March, L. 2, 84–7, 118
Marcuse, H. 112
Marinetti, F.T. 51
Marx, K. 18, 102, 109
maxim of pragmatism 104
meaning 15, 18–20, 30, **42**, 88, 104, 108, 110
meaningless 39, 106
Meillassoux, Q. 98–9
melancholy 31, 36, 40, 51
metaphor 25, 43–4, 58–60, 88, 91
method, and logic 70–3, 87; see also design method
modernism 19, 77, 103
monism 54, 91
murder 61–3

name 10, 23, 104
nature 74–6, 90–1, 93–9, 119
nature semiotics 90
neo-Marxism 18, 101

Nöth, W. 10, 15, 20, 87, 94–6, 119
noise 52, 58

object 21–4, 29–35, 38–9, **40**, **42**, 43–5, **45**, 50–1; and index 62–7, 115–16
object–index relationship 64, 67, 70
object-quality relationship 98
Ogden, C.K. 56

pansemiotics 7, 94–6, 99
parole 17, 116
Peirce, C.S.: education 5; personal life 6; as radical thinker 9, 110; relevance to architecture 1–5; his theory of signs 20–3; work life 5–6
Perez-Gomez, A. 90
phenomenology 98, 101–2, 110, 115
photograph 22, **40**, 62, 77–8, 115
physicality 58–60
Piaget, J. 19
Plato 10
positivism, *see* logical positivism
post-digital 59
posthuman 98–9
poststructuralism 18–19, 112, 116
practice 2, 80, 102, 108–9
practice-led research 102
pragmatism 2, 101–9
primitive hut 27, 106
Preziosi, D. 3, 118
Prolog 72
proof 67–9, 71
Psychometrics Centre, Cambridge 75

qualisign 31, **40**, **42**, **45**, 116
quality 7, 31, **40**, **42**, 43–4, 58; and object 98; raw 41

radical thinking 110, 112–13
reason 103, 107; abductive 80–2, 86, 114; analytic 85; deductive 88; evidential 73; inductive, 86; mathematical 68
referent 21, 23, 26, 59, 116
reflection in action 102
responsive architecture 78
rhematic iconic legisign **40**, 46
rhematic iconic qualisign **40**, 46
rhematic iconic sinsign **40**, 46
rhematic indexical legisign 34, 37, **40**, 50
rhematic indexical sinsign **40**, 46
rhematic symbol 63, 88
rhematic symbolic legisign 36–7, **41**
rheme 34–6, **42**, 43–4, **45**, 82, 116
Richards, I.A. 56
Ricoeur, P. 18
Rorty, R. 8, 101
rule 34, **42**, 45, 63–5, 71–3, 86, 114; breaking 48; of inference 37, **41**; syntactic 36–7
Ruskin, J. 99
Russolo, L. 51

Sagrada Familia 49
satellite imagery 80
Saussure, F. de 5, 7, 11–15, 17–18, 28
Schön, D.A. 102–3
science of design 103

Sebeok, T.A. 23, 90, 93–4
secondness 44–5
semiotics 116; history 10–12; and Peirce 7–9, 20; and de Saussure 15; *see also* sign; sign-situation; Saussure; ten classes of signs
Sherlock Holmes 86
sign 116; and architecture 27–8; history of 10–11, 20; and nature 91–4; situation 7, 30, 37–8, **42**, 64; ten classes of 37–41; vehicle 29, 31, 38, **40**, **42**, **45**, 117; *see also* language; semiotics
signal, 23
signified 14–15, 22, 29, 116
signifier 14–15, 18, 20, 22, 29, 116–17
signs and facts 61
Simon, H. 103, 107
sinsign 32, 39, **40**, **42**, **45**, 117
smart city 74, 78
smoke as sign *see* fire
social media 74–5
sound 27, 117: and difference 15; image 14; materiality of 52; as sinsign 51; and space 35; *see also* explosion; noise
speculative realism 20, 98
Stirling, J. 78
street crier 35–6
sublime 36, 40
syllogism 64–5, 71, 84–5
symbol 36–7
symptom 21
Szerszynski, B. 5, 97–8

Taj Mahal 21, 31–2, 71, 73, 85–6
Tanizaki, Junichiro 84
ten classes of signs 37–41
tetractys 54
thirdness 45–6, 48, 114
transportation system 74
tree as referent 12–15, 29
triadic thinking 4, 52, 54, 106
triadomania 4
Tschumi, B. 61, 112
Twain, M. 60
Twitter 75–6
typologic design 26–7, 32

utilitarianism 102
Utzon, J. 60

value 77, 80, 84, 88, 110
van Eyck, A. 19
Vienna Circle 104, 106
Venn, J. 69
verification 104, 106–7, 111
verification principle 106–7
Vitruvius, P. 53–4, 70

Walther, E. 39
weathervane as sign 12–13, 29–31, 33, **40**, 117
White, H. 109
Wittgenstein, L. 30

zeroness 108

For Product Safety Concerns and Information please contact our EU representative GPSR@taylorandfrancis.com
Taylor & Francis Verlag GmbH, Kaufingerstraße 24, 80331 München, Germany

www.ingramcontent.com/pod-product-compliance
Lightning Source LLC
Chambersburg PA
CBHW070310230426
43664CB00015B/2702